# ACTIVATE YOUR ENGLISH

## Pre-intermediate Coursebook

**Barbara Sinclair**

CAMBRIDGE
UNIVERSITY PRESS

Published by the Press Syndicate of the University of Cambridge
The Pitt Building, Trumpington Street, Cambridge CB2 1RP
40 West 20th Street, New York, NY10011–4211, USA
10 Stamford Road, Oakleigh, Melbourne 3166, Australia

© Cambridge University Press 1995

First published 1995

Printed in Great Britain at
the University Press, Cambridge

ISBN   0 521 42568 9   Coursebook
ISBN   0 521 42569 7   Self-study Workbook
ISBN   0 521 42570 0   Teacher's Book
ISBN   0 521 42571 9   Class Cassette
ISBN   0 521 42572 7   Self-study Workbook Cassette
ISBN   0 521 48401 4   Self-study Workbook CD

# INTRODUCTION

Welcome to *Activate Your English*, a short course at pre-intermediate level. It will help you:

activate the English you have learnt but have forgotten

improve your knowledge of English vocabulary and grammar

feel more confident about understanding and using English in real life

find out more about how to learn English successfully.

The course consists of a Coursebook, a Self-study Workbook and a Self-study Workbook Cassette or CD. For the teacher there is a Teacher's Book and a Class Cassette.

## Coursebook

This is for use in class, and has material for about 40 sessions (of between 45 and 60 minutes). The 20 units have activities to help your speaking, listening, reading and writing skills, and to improve your vocabulary and grammar.

In each unit there is a section called 'It's your choice!' where you can choose activities you would like to do to practise your English. There are also 'Activate your grammar' sections to remind you of important grammar rules, and 'Activate your language' sections to help you remember useful vocabulary and expressions.

The course also helps you find out more about the way you learn English, so that you can be a better learner. 'Learning tips' throughout the course ask you to think about what you are learning and how you are learning.

There are four Review units which help you remember the language covered and evaluate your progress as you go through the course.

At the back of the book you will find a Grammar Review, which gives you more information about the grammar in the course, an Answer Key and Tapescripts for the listening exercises.

## Self-study Workbook

This is for self-study outside class. It is very important because it offers 15–20 hours of further practice and revision of the language and skills covered in the Coursebook.

You will also need the Self-study Workbook Cassette or CD, which has listening and speaking practice activities for you to try on your own.

At the back of the Self-study Workbook you will find an Answer Key and Tapescripts.

I hope you enjoy activating your English!

*Barbara Sinclair*

Barbara Sinclair

# MAP OF THE COURSEBOOK

**Special note**

**Skills:**
For details of skills contents, please see the individual units. The most important skill in the course is **speaking**, and this is practised in every unit. All units contain work on either reading or **listening**, or sometimes on both. there is a balance of skills work between the Coursebook and the Self-study Workbook, so that units that do not, for example, contain any listening work in the Coursebook will have it in the Self-study Workbook.

**Pronunciation**
The course focuses on pronunciation, stress and intonation in special practice activities in both the Coursebook and the Self-study Workbook.

**Learner training**
All units focus on practice in self-direction, and also activity evaluation and/or self-assessment. The map below focuses on other specific areas of learner training.

**Grammar**
Review of present simple: questions, positive and negative statements.

**Vocabulary**
Nationalities, countries, occupations.

**Learner training**
Introduction to self-direction; vocabulary learning strategy: grouping; activity evaluation.

**Speaking**
Asking and talking about names, nationalities, jobs etc.

**Listening**
Listening for specific information.

## 1
### Getting to know you

Find out about the people in your class. What are their names? Where do they come from? What do they do?

## 2
### Vocabulary

Make a list of new words (e.g. countries and nationalities).

Do you know how to pronounce them?

Which words do you want to learn? Put them in groups to help you remember them. Tell the class how you grouped them.

## 3
### Link up

Work with a partner and think of some more questions Susan and Wolfgang can ask each other. Can you guess their answers?

Listen to the cassette: are you right?

## Activate your grammar

**Questions in the present simple**

| | | |
|---|---|---|
| **Are** | **you** | **German?** |
| **Is** | **he/she** | **Malaysian?** |
| | | |
| **Do** | **you** | **come here often?** |
| **Does** | **he/she** | |
| | | |
| **Where do** | **you** | **come from?** |
| **does** | **he/she** | |
| | | |
| **What do** | **you** | **do?** |
| **does** | **he/she** | |

➡ **See Grammar Review 1 on page 74.**

# 4
## When we say hello

*'In Germany we shake hands.'*

*'In Japan we bow.'*

What about you? Discuss and show different ways of greeting that you know about.

# 5
## It's your choice!

In 'It's your choice!' sections of this book you can find different activities to do.

You can choose *what* you want to do. Choose an activity you think is useful and interesting. You can learn better if you do something you want to do.

You can choose *how* you want to do it. You can work alone or with someone else. People like to work in different ways.

You can say *what you think* about the activity. You can discover what activities you like and don't like. This can help you know more about how you learn.

Look at these activities and choose one to do.

### a)  True or false?

Write about a person in your class. Write some things which are true and some things which are not true.

Feedback: Read your description to the class. Can they say which parts are true and which parts are not true?

### b)  Who is it?

Write about a person in your class, but do not give his or her name.

Feedback: Read your description to the class. Can they guess who it is?

### c)  About yourself

Write about yourself. Show your writing to your teacher. Make any corrections and stick a photo of yourself on it. Put it on the classroom wall when it is finished.

### d)  Useful words

Make a list of useful words that you want to learn from this unit, such as jobs. Try to learn them now. Test yourself.

Write your words on a sheet of paper. Make photocopies for the class or put it on the classroom wall.

# 6
## Feedback

Fill in the feedback box below, on the activities in Exercise 5. Tick (✓) where appropriate. Discuss your activities with your class and teacher.

| Activity | I did: | Good | OK | Not good |
|---|---|---|---|---|
| a)  True or false? | | | | |
| b)  Who is it? | | | | |
| c)  About yourself | | | | |
| d)  Useful words | | | | |

**In Self-study Workbook Unit 1**
Spelling and pronunciation of nationalities, countries, jobs; questions, dictation, recording new words.

**Grammar**
'Want to', 'need to', 'can'; linking words: 'so', 'so that', 'in order to', 'to', 'because'; 'for' + noun; 'by -ing'.

**Speaking**
Asking about and giving reasons for learning English, saying what you want to, need to and can do; saying what you can do to improve your English.

**Listening**
Listening for specific information.

**Learner training**
Practice in self-direction; reasons for learning; different ways to improve language skills; activity evaluation.

2

# 1
## Why do you want to learn English?

*'I want to learn English because it's a very important language for tourism in my country.'*
*Elena, hotel receptionist, Greece*

Why do you want to learn English? Is it mostly for:

a) work?          c) study?

b) travel?        d) other reasons?

How many people can you find in your class who want to learn English for the same reason as you? Form a group with them and discuss your reasons in more detail.

What is the most common reason in your class? What is the most unusual reason?

# 2
## What can you do?

What languages can you do the following in?

Say a few words, such as 'hello', 'goodbye', 'please', 'thank you'

Say who you are and where you come from

Talk about your family

Go shopping

Order a meal in a restaurant

Talk about what you did yesterday

Explain your work

Understand the news on TV

Understand entertainment programmes or films

Understand the newspapers

Read a novel

Have a conversation about personal things

Understand a native speaker talking at normal speed

Write a business letter

Give a speech

Write poetry

Other: _____

_____

Ask someone else.

Which things are the most difficult to do? Why?

**Activate your grammar**
'Can/can't'

What can you do?
Can you say 'hello' in French?
Yes, I can.
No, I can't.
I can order a meal in Japanese.

➡ See Grammar Review 2 on page 74.

# 3
## What do you need to do in English?

*'I want to learn English because I need it for my job. I'm a waiter in a restaurant in Barcelona, Spain. I need to understand what the tourists say and to explain the menu.'*
*Jordi, waiter, Spain.*

Fill in the checklist for Jordi.

 Listen and fill in the checklist for Manee.

Fill in the checklist for yourself. Then ask someone else and fill in the last column. Do you have the same or different needs?

How can this course help you? Discuss this with your teacher.

| Skill | Jordi needs to: | Manee needs to: | I need to: | _____ needs to: |
|---|---|---|---|---|
| understand | | | | |
| speak | | | | |
| read | | | | |
| write | | | | |
| know vocabulary about | | | | |

## Activate your grammar
### 'Want to/need to'

| I want to<br>She needs to | learn English | so that I/she can …<br>to …<br>in order to … |
|---|---|---|
| I<br>He | don't<br>doesn't | want    to speak English.<br>need    to write English. |
| Why<br>Why<br>What | do you | want to learn English?<br>need to understand English?<br>need to do in English? |

➡ See Grammar Review 3 on page 74.

# 4
## It's your choice!

What can do you to do to improve your English?

Choose one of the following:

Speaking

Understanding (listening)

Writing

Vocabulary

Reading

Grammar

Find other people who have chosen the same topic and form a group. How many ways can you think of to improve your English in this area?

Feedback: Present your ideas to the class. Which ones will you try?

### Activate your language

| To improve your speaking | you can | start an English club.<br>talk in English with a friend. |
| You can improve your writing | by | keeping an English diary.<br>having an English penfriend. |

# 5
## Feedback

What do you think about the activities in this unit?
Tick (✓) your answers.

| Activity | Interesting | Useful | Enjoyable | Other comments? |
|---|---|---|---|---|
| 1  Why do you want to learn English? | | | | |
| 2  What can you do? | | | | |
| 3  What do you need to do in English? | | | | |
| 4  It's your choice! | | | | |

I've got some new ideas for improving my English:  Yes ☐   No ☐

**In Self-study Workbook Unit 2**
Reading comprehension; grammar review: 'so that/because'; reading for specific information; writing: your English language needs.

# 3

## What do you think?

**Grammar**
Review of questions with 'do' and 'does'; 'like/ don't like' + noun/ gerund.

**Vocabulary**
Intensifiers: 'really', 'quite'; adjectives: with '-ed /-ing';

**Speaking**
Asking for and giving opinions; agreeing and disagreeing; intonation practice.

**Listening**
Listening for specific information.

**Learner training**
Practice in self-direction; language awareness; activity evaluation.

## 1

### Do you think the same?

Work with a partner. Find three things you have the same opinions about and three things you have different opinions about.

### Activate your grammar
**Questions with 'do' and 'does'**

| | |
|---|---|
| **Do you like** | **red wine?** **potatoes?** |
| **Does she like** | **drinking alcohol?** **cycling?** |
| **Yes, I do.** | **No, I don't.** |
| **Yes, she does.** | **No, she doesn't.** |
| **What do you think** **How do you feel** | **about violence on TV?** |

 **See Grammar Review 1 on page 74.**

## 2

### Saying what you think

Here are some expressions for saying whether you like or don't like something. Put them in a list: start with the most positive (+++++) and finish with the most negative (-----). Use 'n' for 'neutral' (you don't like it or hate it).

| | |
|---|---|
| I hate it. | I like it. |
| I really hate it. | I love it. |
| I like it very much. | I don't like it. |
| I'm not sure. | I don't like it at all. |
| I quite like it. | I don't like it very much. |
| I really love it. | |

## 3

### Greg and Linda in Singapore

Greg is American and Linda is British. They are both teacher trainers and live and work in Singapore.

We interviewed them to find out what they think about living in Singapore.

a) Can you guess what they like and what they don't like?

b) Choose three of the topics from the chart below.

Listen to the interview and put plus signs (+) or minus signs (-) in the boxes to show what Greg and Linda think about the three topics you have chosen. The first one has been done for you.

**+++++** really loves it/them
**n** neutral (doesn't like or hate it/them)
**-----** really hates it/them

| Topic | Linda | Greg |
|---|---|---|
| the weather | ++++ | + |
| the skyscrapers | | |
| the people | | |
| the food | | |
| the night life | | |
| the plant life | | |
| the shops | | |
| the beaches | | |

Work in a group and compare answers.

c) Work with a partner. What do you think of the place where you live now? Why?

## 4

### Vocabulary

a) What do you think about nude sunbathing? Why do you think that?

b) How many words do you know for describing things you like or things you don't like? Work in a group and compare your lists.

c) Work with a partner. Ask each other what you think about the following and why:

flying long distances     jazz

eating Chinese food

### Activate your grammar
**Adjectives**

| | |
|---|---|
| It's disgusting. | I'm disgusted (by it). |
| It's boring. | I'm bored (by it). |

➡ See Grammar Review 4 on page 75.

## 6

### Discussion: the best place to live!

*'I think the best place to live is Dublin because the people are friendly.'*

*'You're kidding! I think the best place to live is Tahiti because ...'*

Work in a group. Your teacher will give you each a card. Express the idea on your card and give reasons. Try to win the argument.

## 5

### Agreeing and disagreeing

*'I think New York is a really exciting city.'*

What do you think. Why?

Listen to the phrases from 'Activate your language' and practise saying them.

### Activate your language

| | |
|---|---|
| Yes, so do I. | Yes, but it's |
| Mmm, I agree. | very dangerous. |
| Yes, me too. | I disagree. |
| Yes, I do too. | No, it's not! |
| I think so, too. | You're kidding! |

# 7
## It's your choice!

Choose one of the topics below. What do you think about it and why?

| | | |
|---|---|---|
| having children | keeping pets | men |
| smoking in public places | cars | women |
| | male drivers | |

Find other people who want to discuss the topic and form a group. Do you all agree?

# 8
## What do you think about learning English?

Discuss these questions:

a) Do you like learning English? Why?/ Why not?

b) What do you think about this book? Why?

c) What classroom activities do you like best? Why?

# 9
## Feedback

What do you think about the activities in this unit? Write plus (+) or minus (–) signs to show your opinions.

| Activity | +/– |
|---|---|
| 1  Do you think the same? | |
| 2  Saying what you think | |
| 3  Greg and Linda in Singapore | |
| 4  Vocabulary | |
| 5  Agreeing and disagreeing | |
| 6  Discussion: the best place to live! | |
| 7  It's your choice! | |
| 8  What do you think about learning English? | |

**In Self-study Workbook Unit 3** Word-building: adjectives with '-ed/-ing'; reading comprehension; intonation practice; how to keep a phrase book.

**Grammar**
Prepositions of location; practice in question formation.

**Vocabulary**
Adjectives to describe places, facilities, attractions; points of the compass.

**Speaking**
Asking about and describing places.

**Listening**
Listening for specific information – people talking about their home towns.

**Reading**
Reading for specific information – a travel handbook.

**Learner training**
Practice in self-direction; dictionary skills: identifying stressed syllables; activity evaluation.

# 1

## Where is that?

a) We asked people about their home towns. Before you listen to the cassette, look at the pictures. Do you know anything about Cairns, Bath or Yakima?

Do you know what countries they are in?

What do you think they are like?

Now listen to the cassette to find out about these places.

**Activate your language**

It's north of the city.

It's to the south of the lake.

It's in the west of the country.

| It's | situated | in the eastern | part of the town. |
| | located | western | |
| | | southern | |
| | | northern | |

I live in Cairns.

We come from Bath.

My home's in Yakima.

Map of Bali

Map of Brazil

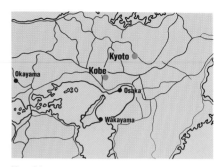

Map of Japan

b) Look at the maps above and describe the location of the following places:

| | | |
|---|---|---|
| Denpasar | Fortaleza | Kyoto |
| Kobe | Kuta | Recife |

c) *'My house is in the western part of the village in the road opposite the church. It's close to the park and not far from the forest. My favourite part of the village is the park next to the church.'*

Work with a partner or in a group. Talk about the location of:

your home city, town or village – or your favourite part of it

your house or flat.

## Activate your language
### Prepositions of location

| | |
|---|---|
| near | by |
| next to | in |
| beside | on |
| close to | above |
| not far from | under |
| opposite | below |

# 2
## What's it like?

'Where is it?' 'What is it famous for?' 'Where does it get its name from?'

Work in a group. What other questions can you ask about a place? Make a list.

Read the text on Kandy in Sri Lanka. How many answers did you find?

Make a list of any new words you want to learn.

---

**Kandy, Sri Lanka**

Kandy is situated in the foothills of the Hill Country on the banks of a lovely tree-lined lake. It gets its name from the Sinhalese word *kanda*, which means hill. The city is 488 metres above sea level and so it is a cool place for its 100,000 inhabitants to live. It is a cultural and religious centre and is famous for a number of buildings, such as the Temple of the Tooth which houses one of Buddha's teeth. There are also important Buddhist and Hindu shrines, two museums, botanical gardens and an arts and crafts centre. You can see the famous Kandyan dancers performing fire dances and walking on burning coals and you can watch elephants being bathed in the Mahaweli River, the longest river in Sri Lanka.

# 3
## Vocabulary: describing places

Work with a partner. For each word listed below, use a dictionary to help you find out the meaning and mark the stressed syllable.

crowded            suburban

multi-racial       industrial

high-rise          agricultural

rural              urban

> some countries. • *The area depends on agriculture for most of its income.* • *70% of the country's population practises subsistence agriculture.* • Compare HORTICULTURE.
> **ag·ri·cul·tur·al** /ˌæg·rɪˈkʌl·tʃˀrˑˀl, $-tʃɚˑˀl/ *adj* • *He said that the world's supply of agricultural land is shrinking fast, and every year produces less food.* • *She's studying agricultural science.* • *The country's economy is mainly agricultural* (= based on farming) *and depends on crops like coffee.*
> **a·ground** /əˈgraʊnd/ *adj* [after v], *adv* [not gradable] (of a boat or ship) touching the ground or, where there is little water, touching the bottom of the sea, a lake, etc. and therefore unable to move • *The ship is currently aground off the Brittany coast.* • *The oil tanker ran/went aground on a mud bank in thick fog.* • (fig.) *The plans to send aid to the areas worst affected by the fighting have* **run** *aground* (= stopped because of difficulties).
> **ah** /ɑː/, **aah** *exclamation* used to express understanding, pleasure, pain, surprise or the fact that you have noticed something • *Ah yes, now I see what's wrong – the wires have come loose.* • *Ah, it's wonderful to see you again.* • *Ah, that's terrible, you must have been in such pain.* • *Why has the train stopped. Ah, now we're off again.* • *Ah, Jessica, I'm glad you could make it.*
> **a·ha** /ɑːˈhɑː/ *exclamation* used to express understanding of something being said or satisfaction at suddenly finding or understanding something • *"And this is the main computer?" "Aha."* • *Aha, now I've got you – you can't escape.*
> **ah·choo** /əˈtʃuː/ *exclamation Am for* ATISHOO
> **a·head** [IN FRONT] /əˈhed/ *adv* [not gradable] (directly) in front • *The road ahead looks rather busy – shall we turn off and go a different way?* • *Turn left at the traffic lights, and you'll see the hospital* **straight** *ahead.* • *We slowed down, to let the other cars get ahead of us.* • *I'm on the waiting list for a ticket, but there are ten people ahead of me.* • *Ahead also means in a more advanced position: The Prime Minister's speech* **put** *his party 5% ahead in the opinion polls.* • *If*

Do the same for the new words from the text about Kandy.

Find out more words you need to describe the place you are from or the place where you live now.

# 4
## It's your choice!

Choose one of the following activities:

**Speaking**

With a partner: ask and talk in detail about where you come from or where you live now.

**Reading**

On your own or with a partner: read a tourist brochure and note down interesting facts and new words you want to learn.

**Speaking**

With a partner or in a small group: talk about places you recommend for a holiday.

**Writing**

On your own: write about a place you know well. Describe it in detail.

# 5
## Feedback

What do you think about the activities in this unit?
Tick (✔) your answers and give reasons.

| Activity | Useful | Enjoyable | Interesting | Why? |
|---|---|---|---|---|
| 1a | | | | |
| 1b | | | | |
| 1c | | | | |
| 2 | | | | |
| 3 | | | | |
| 4 | | | | |

# 5

## The people in your life

**Grammar**
Comparisons.

**Vocabulary**
For describing people's appearance, qualities, interests and other information.

**Speaking**
Describing people and relationships.

**Reading**
Skimming and scanning: a description of a person.

**Learner training**
Reading strategies: skimming and scanning; practice in self-direction; activity evaluation.

## 1

### Who's who in your life?

Who are the most important people in your life? Why?
Discuss this with a partner.

Do you think family members are more important than friends?
Why?/Why not?

1. Don my husband.

2. My mother.

3. Linda, my boss.

4. Richard, my neighbour.

## 2

### My brother, Nick

a) What can you say about Nick?

Look at the photo of Nick.
What can you say about him?

Read the text quickly to get some ideas about him.

**Learning tip**

**Skimming**

This is what you do when you read quickly to get the main ideas of a text; for example, when you read a newspaper article or a novel.

**Activate your language**

| He looks | nice. |
| | like me. |
| | like a police officer. |

My brother, Nick, is a motor mechanic. He's three years younger than me. He's got his own business and lives near Brentwood in Essex in the south-east of England. He's 37, married and has got three cats, but no children. He's not very tall, but he's taller than me, and has got reddish-brown hair and brown eyes like me. He looks like me, but he's got a moustache and wears glasses. He's quite muscular and very fit. He's kind and generous and a very good cook. Generally, he's very easy-going and humorous. He likes animals, swimming and parachuting and tells good jokes. He's important to me because he's my only brother and we get on well.

**Activate your grammar**

**Comparisons**

| He's | younger | than me. |
| | taller | |

➡ See Grammar Review 5 on page 75.

b) What do you know about Nick?

Read these questions and then look at the text to find the answers.

**Information**
How old is he?
Is he married?

**Appearance**
How tall is he?
What colour hair
 has he got?

**Qualities**
What is he like?
Is he generous?
Is he kind?

**Interests**
What are his
 hobbies?
What does he like?
What does he like
 doing?

**Learning tip**
**Scanning**

This what you do when you look quickly at a text to find specific information, for example, when you look up a name and telephone number in a telephone book, or a detail you want to know from a text.

**Activate your grammar**
'Have got/has got'

I've got        brown hair.
She's got

See Grammar Review 6 on page 75.

c) Vocabulary development

Work with a partner or in a group. Put the words below into the following categories:
Information, Appearance, Qualities, Interests.

| | | |
|---|---|---|
| brunette | widow | mid-thirties |
| divorced | Londoner | cinema |
| slim | handsome | beard |
| single | football | nosey |
| sporty | cheerful | intelligent |
| blonde | hard-working | red-haired |
| bad-tempered | well-built | friendly |

# 3
## It's your choice! (1)
**What do they look like?**

Choose one of the people in the photos. Find words or phrases you can use to describe him or her. You can choose to work alone or with someone else.

Present your descriptions to the class.

Make a note of new words you want to learn from any of the categories.

# 4
## It's your choice! (2)
### What are they like?

Choose one of these activities.

**Speaking**

Talk about people who are very important to you and say why.

**Writing**

Write about someone who is very important to you.

# 5
## Feedback

What do you think about the activities in this unit? Why?

| Activity | Very easy | Easy | OK | Difficult | Very difficult | Why? |
|---|---|---|---|---|---|---|
| 1 | | | | | | |
| 2a | | | | | | |
| 2b | | | | | | |
| 2c | | | | | | |
| 3 | | | | | | |
| 4 | | | | | | |

**Tick (✓) your answer**

| Reading strategy | Yes | No | Not sure |
|---|---|---|---|
| I know what skimming is | | | |
| I know what scanning is | | | |

**In Self-study
Workbook Unit 5**
Vocabulary development:
word pairs, opposites;
listening comprehension;
stress and pronunciation
practice.

**Score**

1 International
  Night at Link Up

2 Nice to meet
  you!

3 I love it!
  I hate it!

## A

## Progress check

Do the following activities to check your progress.

### 1  International Night at Link Up

a)  How many countries and nationalities can you write correctly in two minutes? Check your spellings.

*Give yourself one point for each correctly spelt word.*

b)  It's International Night at Link Up. What kind of music, food etc. do you want? Plan the best and the worst International Night you can think of! Complete the 'best' and 'worst' posters below.

*Give yourself 1 point for each correctly spelt word. Up to 5 bonus points can be given by the class for good plans.*

### 2  Nice to meet you!

Work with a partner. Each of you should choose a name, a nationality and a job (but don't tell each other what they are before you start).

You meet for the first time at Link Up. Introduce yourselves and start a conversation. How long can you keep talking? Time yourselves.

*Give yourselves 5 points each for every minute your conversation lasts.*

### 3  I love it! I hate it!

Discuss the two topics below with a partner:

a)  British food

b)  Holidays with the family

Partner A loves British food, but hates holidays with the family. Partner B hates British food, but loves holidays with the family. How long can you keep talking? Time yourselves.

*Give yourselves 10 points each for every minute your conversations last.*

## 4  Where is it?

Think of three well-known places and where they are. Work with a partner and tell each other the names of your places and where they are.

*Give your partner 0–5 points for each correct answer. The more detailed the answer, the more points you should give.*

## 5  People

a)  Write a description of the person in the picture.

b)  Write a description of:

your ideal neighbour

your ideal husband or wife or partner

Give your writing to someone else to check.

*Start with 25 points for each piece of writing. Take off 1 point for every mistake. Now, for each piece of writing, add up to 15 bonus points for length and detail. Discuss your score with your checker.*

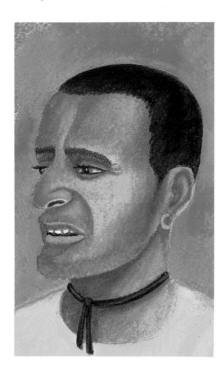

# B
## Checklist

Use this checklist to record how you feel about your progress.

| I can | yes/no |
|---|---|
| introduce myself | |
| talk about where I come from | |
| talk about my work | |
| talk about my family and friends | |
| say what I think about things | |
| agree with other people | |
| disagree with other people | |
| say what I want or need to do | |
| say where a place is | |
| describe what people look like | |
| describe what people are like | |

| I know | yes/no |
|---|---|
| some useful phrases for polite conversation | |
| a lot about the people in my class | |
| the difference between skimming and scanning when I read | |
| how to use a dictionary to find out the stress of a word | |
| some different ways of storing and learning vocabulary | |
| which learning activities I like best | |

# C
## Personal plan

What problems do you have and how do you plan to help yourself?

**Problems**

**Plans**

## Score

4  Where is it?

5  People

**Now add up your total score**

200–270  Brilliant!
150–199  Very good.
100–149  Satisfactory. Don't forget to review the units.
0–99     You need to review Units 1–5 again.

# 1

## Is your life stressful?

Tick (✓) the things you do every day:

☐ work for 10 or more hours

☐ do the shopping

☐ prepare meals for others

☐ care for a sick or elderly relative

☐ travel for more than two hours

☐ look after a child or children

☐ sleep for less than six hours

☐ do housework

Is your daily life stressful?

Work with a partner and compare lists. What other things make life stressful? Who has the most stressful life? Why?

# 2

## Louise

Read about Louise. How stressful is her life? Why?

# Time for yourself?

Stress is a big problem today. Our lives are busy. Do we have enough time for ourselves? Louise Brent, a gym instructor in a large health club in London and divorced with one child, Joanne, tells us about her day.

Joey, who's two and a half now, always wakes up early – at about 6 o'clock, so I get up then. I wash and dress her and give her breakfast. Then she plays and I get ready for work. I eat some muesli, have a quick cup of coffee and then at 7.30 I drive her to the child-minder.

I catch the 8.15 train to Cannon Street and usually start work at 9 am. In my lunch break from 1 to 2 o'clock I usually go shopping and then eat a sandwich in a cafe.

I finish work at 6, catch the 6.20 train and fetch Joey from the child-minder an hour later. We get home at about 8 o'clock. Joey eats at the child-minder's, so we play together for half an hour and then I put her to bed. I eat something – usually something quick like pasta or a frozen TV dinner – at about 9, watch the 10 o'clock news and go to bed at 10.30.

I spend more time with Joey at the weekend. We sometimes go to the park or the zoo or I invite other mothers with their children to visit us. When she's in bed, I do the housework. It's very tiring, but one weekend a month she goes to her father, who is now married to someone else. That's when I get some time for myself.

**Louise and Joanne Brent**

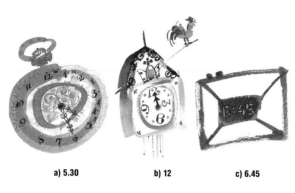

a) 5.30          b) 12          c) 6.45          d) 1.01

# 4

## Have you got the time?

How many ways can you say the following times?

a) 5.30     b) 12     c) 6.45     d) 1.01

**Activate your language**
**What's the time?**

**2.15 pm/14.15**
It's two fifteen pm.
It's two fifteen in the afternoon.
It's a quarter past two in the afternoon.

# 3

## Louise's schedule

Write the questions for these answers:

a) At about 6 am.
b) She drives to the child-minder.
c) At about 8 o'clock.
d) At the weekend.
e) She eats a sandwich.
f) She eats pasta.
g) Between 1 and 2 o'clock.
h) At 6.20 pm.
i) For half an hour.
j) At 10.30 pm.

**Activate your grammar**
**Present simple for habitual actions**

**Statements**

| I | usually | wake up | early. |
| Joey | always | wakes up | |
| We | | wake up | |
| They | | wake up | |

| I | don't | usually | wake up | early. |
| Joey | doesn't | | | |
| We | don't | | | |
| They | don't | | | |

➡ See Grammar Review 7 on page 75.

**Questions**

| When | do | you | usually get up? |
| What time | does | he | |

| What | do | you | usually do at the weekend? |
| | does | she | |

| Why | do | you | get up early every day? |

| How | do | you | usually get to work? |

| Do | you | usually get up early? |
| Does | he | |

Yes, I do.          No, he doesn't.

➡ See Grammar Review 8 on page 76.

# 5

## What do you usually do?

What do you usually do on Mondays in a typical working week? Make a chart like the one below and fill it in.

Work with a partner. Ask about what your partner usually does on Mondays. Fill in the details and compare your days.

| Time (am) | Activity | |
|---|---|---|
| | I usually… | Yoko usually… |
| 12.00–12.30 | Sleep | watches TV |
| 1.00–1.30 | Sleep | goes to bed |

| Time (pm) | Activity | |
|---|---|---|
| | I usually… | Yoko usually… |
| 12.00–12.30 | have lunch | goes shopping |
| 1.00–1.30 | have lunch | has lunch |

Now talk about your typical week. What do you do on Tuesdays, Thursdays etc.? What do you do at the weekend? How much time for yourself do you have in a week? What do you do then?

**Activate your grammar**
**Reflexives**

| I have no time for | myself |
| You have no time for | yourself/yourselves |
| He has no time for | himself |
| She has no time for | herself |
| We have no time for | ourselves |
| They have no time for | themselves |

# 6
## Always … never

most
frequent

least
frequent

always

never

Put these words in the right place
on the diagram above:

sometimes    often    rarely    usually

# 7
## It's your choice! (1)

Choose one of the activities. You
can work alone or in a pair or group.

### a) Vocabulary

How many other words or phrases
can you find to say how frequently
you do something?

Show their meanings in a diagram
like the one in Exercise 6.

### b) Sentence patterns

Make as many correct sentences
from these words as you can:

go    the    we    sometimes

to    Sundays    on    cinema

Make similar sentences using
the words in Exercise 6. Use a
grammar book to help you or talk
to your teacher.

What conclusions do you come to?

# 8
## It's your choice! (2)

Choose one of the activities below.

### Speaking

Work in a group. Talk about five
things you *never* do and why.

### Class survey

Work with a partner or in a group.
Choose your own topic and do a
class survey about people's habits.
For example, how long do they
sleep? What do they do at the
weekends or in the evenings?

### Writing

Write about a typical day or week
in your life or someone else's life.

# 9
## Feedback

What do you think about the activities in this unit? Tick (✓) your answers
and give reasons.

| Activity | Useful | Enjoyable | Interesting | Why? |
|----------|--------|-----------|-------------|------|
| 1 | | | | |
| 2 | | | | |
| 3 | | | | |
| 4 | | | | |
| 5 | | | | |
| 6 | | | | |
| 7 | | | | |
| 8 | | | | |

**In Self-study
Workbook Unit 6**
Listening comprehension;
grammar check: word
order; making a learning
schedule; making a
grammar pattern book.

# 7 An interesting life?

**Grammar**
Simple past: regular and irregular forms, negatives.

**Reading**
Practice in skimming and scannning.

**Speaking**
Talking about your life; pronunciation of verb endings in simple past.

**Vocabulary**
Regular and irregular verbs; dates.

**Learner training**
Practice in self-direction; how to make a verb bank; activity/self-evaluation.

## 1

### My life, by Bernard Hoehner

a)  Look at the photo. What nationality do you think Bernard is?

Read about Bernard's life. Is it an interesting life? Why?

b)  The following are *key words* because they are important for understanding the text. What do the words mean?

immigrant          sheriff          veterinary medicine

veterinarian          reservation

Mark the stressed syllables. How are these words pronounced?

Look again at the text. Are there any more words you want to find out about?

c)  Work with a partner. What do you think were the three most interesting things or events in Bernard's life? Why?

## 2

### The simple past

The underlined verbs in these sentences are in the simple past:

My dad <u>was</u> sheriff of Wakpala.

We <u>didn't</u> have electricity.

I <u>worked</u> in Boston as a veterinarian for one year.

Underline all the verbs in the simple past in the text about Bernard Hoehner.

I was born on March 25th, 1924, on Standing Rock Indian Reservation in Wakpala, South Dakota, in the US. My dad, a German immigrant, was the Sheriff of Wakpala. He had a horse and a gun and a badge and all. My mom was a Sioux Indian. We were very poor. We didn't have electricity, telephones or running water on the reservation.

When I was young I learned a lot about animals, especially horses, from my Sioux relatives – how to ride them, how to break them, what to do if they were sick. At home we spoke English and Lakhota, the language of the Sioux Indians.

I started school in 1929 and graduated from Wakpala High School in 1941. Then I left the reservation and joined the Marines and fought in the South Pacific. In 1945 I went to live in California, near Los Angeles. I met Evelyn and we got married in 1946. From 1947 to 1952 I studied Veterinary Medicine in college. In 1947 my first son, Tony, was born. Then in 1950 and 1952 my daughters Nancy and Margaret were born.

I worked in Boston as a veterinarian for one year and then in San Mateo in California for six years. We had two more sons, Greg and Mark. In 1959 we moved to Walnut Creek near San Francisco and I became a partner in an animal hospital. I retired in 1989. Evelyn and I still live in Walnut Creek.

## Activate your grammar

**Simple past: regular verbs**

The verbs which end in '-ed' in the simple past (e.g. 'learned') are regular verbs.

| Infinitive | Simple past |
|---|---|
| to work | worked |
| to start | started |
| to learn | learned |
| to play | played |

| | | |
|---|---|---|
| I | worked | hard yesterday. |
| You | started | work early today. |
| He/She | learned | French at school. |
| We | played | tennis on Saturday. |
| They | played | football last year. |

See Grammar Review 9 on page 76.

**Simple past: irregular verbs**

Some verbs do not end in '-ed' in the simple past (e.g. 'I am' – 'I was'). These are irregular verbs.

| Infinitive | Simple past |
|---|---|
| to be | was/were |
| to see | saw |
| to go | went |
| to think | thought |

| | | |
|---|---|---|
| I | was | there last week. |
| They | were | in Paris on Wednesday. |
| I | saw | him yesterday. |
| We | went | to the cinema last night. |
| He | thought | about the problem all day. |

See Grammar Review 10 on page 76.

## Learning tip
**How to learn irregular verbs**

Make a verb bank for irregular verbs.

Group irregular verbs with similar patterns together to make them easier to remember.

Your dictionary will probably have the simple past form of any irregular verb and a list at the back.

bring brought
teach taught
think thought
fight fought

## 3
### It's your choice! (1)
**More about Bernard**

Choose one of the topics below:

| Lakhota | Life on the reservation | Being a veterinarian |
|---|---|---|

Now listen to Bernard talking on the cassette and make notes on your chosen topic as you listen.

## 4
### Test yourself

Sai Song has problems with the simple past.
Correct her mistakes with verbs in the work below.

> I am born in 1947 in Shanghai. In 1950 my parents bring me and my 3 brothers to Taiwan to live. We live in Kaohsiung, near the sea. My mother and father, now dead, make prawn mee (noodles) and sell it to workers in the town. It is hard life. I do not go to school until I am 10. I study very hard and get a job in a shop when I am 16. On March 1966 I get married to Harry. We get flat in town. Harry is sailor. His parents coming from Beijing in 1932. 9 April 1970 we have son, Kelvin. Last year we travel to Australia and New Zealand. We like it very much.

Did you notice any other mistakes? What were they? Can you correct them?

### Activate your language

| We saw it | yesterday |
|---|---|
| | last night/week/month/year |
| | on Monday |
| | on 9th June, 1995 |
| | at the weekend |
| | in May |
| | in 1976 |

# 5
## Tell me about yourself

Work with a partner. Tell each other about your lives, like Bernard and Sai Song.

# 6
## It's your choice! (2)

Choose the activity you want to do. You can work alone or with someone else.

### a) Speaking

Work with a partner. Tell each other about something interesting you did last week.

### b) Vocabulary and grammar

Start your verb bank. Use a dictionary to help you.

### c) Writing

Write about an interesting or important time in your life. When was it? What happened?

# 7
## Feedback

What do you think about the activities in this unit? Why?

| Activity | Very easy | Easy | OK | Difficult | Very difficult | Why? |
|---|---|---|---|---|---|---|
| 1a | | | | | | |
| 1b | | | | | | |
| 1c | | | | | | |
| 2 | | | | | | |
| 3 | | | | | | |
| 4 | | | | | | |
| 5 | | | | | | |
| 6 | | | | | | |

In Self-study
**Workbook Unit 7**
Reading comprehension with self-assessment; pronunciation practice.

**Grammar**
Simple past: negatives, questions with 'was/were' and 'did'.

**Speaking**
Asking about the past; apologising; making excuses.

**Listening**
Listening for gist; listening for specific information.

**Vocabulary**
More regular and irregular verbs in the simple past.

**Learner training**
Practice in self-direction; self-assessment; listening strategies.

**What happened?**

8

## 1

### What happened?

 a) Listen to the telephone conversation between Lisa and Joe.

1 What is their relationship?

2 What is their problem?

 b) Listen again.

1 What did Lisa do every day last week?

2 Why did she do it?

3 Who was Steve?

4 What did Steve do on Friday?

5 What happened?

6 How did Joe feel when he heard?

7 How did Lisa feel when he asked the questions? Why?

c) When is 'did' or 'didn't' used in a question in the simple past and when not?

### Activate your grammar

**Simple past: 'wh-' questions**

| What | did | he do? |
| Where | | you go? |
| How | | they feel? |

| Why | were | you late? |
| Who | was | Steve? |

| What | happened? | |

➡ See Grammar Review 11 on page 76.

**Simple past: yes/no questions**

| Did | you see Fred? |
| Didn't | he have a coffee? |

| Yes, | I | did. |
| No, | he | didn't. |

| Were | you | at the cinema? |
| Wasn't | he | with you? |

| Yes, | I | was. |
| No, | he | wasn't. |

➡ See Grammar Review 12 on page 77.

## 2

### Apologies and excuses

a) It's your partner's day off. You want him or her to do some jobs at home.

Work with a partner and choose one list each. Add some more jobs to your list and give it to your partner.

Please do these jobs while I'm out! Thanks!

Clean car    Bath dog
Take kids to park
Fill in Tax Return
Mow lawn    Do washing

Do these jobs for me, please!
See you later!    xxx

Return books to library.
Clean out garage.
Take dog to vet's.
Make birthday cake.
Clean oven.    Do ironing.

Take it in turns to be A and B. A asks questions about the list, and B answers 'No' to all of them. Have a conversation like this:

A: Ask B if he/she did the jobs on the list.
B: Say no and apologise.
A: Ask why not.
B: Make an excuse. Say what you did instead.

b) Listen to the cassette recording of the following phrases:

Er, no. Sorry …

I'm really sorry …

I'm terribly sorry …

No, I damn well didn't!

No, I didn't!

No!

I'm so sorry, I didn't.

Listen to the intonation. In which phrases does the speaker sound really sorry?

Practise saying these.

## 3
### What did you do last week to improve your English?

Work with a partner and discuss these questions about last week.

#### Questionnaire

1  How much English did you speak outside class?

2  Who did you speak to in English?

3  How well did you do when you spoke English?

4  What did you read in English?

5  Did you have any problems while reading? If so, what were they?

6  What TV programmes or films did you see in English?

7  Did you have any problems while listening? If so, what were they?

8  What did you write in English?

9  Did you have any problems while writing? If so, what were they?

10 Did you try to learn any new words? If so, which ones?

11 How often did you review your class notes?

# 4

## It's your choice!

### Class surveys: what did you do last week?

Choose one of the following topics for a class survey and make a list of six questions to ask.

| | | |
|---|---|---|
| television | shopping | eating places visited |
| general leisure activities | exercise and sport | telephone use |

Ask other groups your questions and answer their questions.

Feedback: What did you find out? In your group, collect your results and present them to the class.

# 5

## Listening: how much did you understand?

When you listened to the conversation between Joe and Lisa in Exercise 1, how much did you understand?

What problems did you have, if any? What can you do about them?

### Learning tips

a) **Don't try to hear every word. It's not necessary and it stops you listening for the main ideas.**

Listen to the sentences on the cassette. Can you understand them? Can you hear every word? Did you need to hear every word?

b) **Listen for the stressed words. These are the key words, important for meaning.**

Listen to the sentences on the cassette. Can you understand them? Which words are stressed?

c) **Listen for repeated ideas. People often repeat ideas and sometimes words. Don't worry if you don't hear something: you may get it the second time!**

Listen again to the conversation for Exercise 1. Can you hear the repetitions?

# 6

## Feedback

How well did you do in this unit? Tick (✓) your answers and give reasons.

| Activity | I did very well | I did OK | I didn't do very well | Why? |
|---|---|---|---|---|
| 1 | | | | |
| 2a | | | | |
| 2b | | | | |
| 3 | | | | |
| 4 | | | | |
| 5 | | | | |

**In Self-study Workbook Unit 8** Writing questions in the simple past; reading comprehension; intonation practice; useful phrases.

# 9

## An interesting experience

**Grammar**
More practice in simple past; adjectives and adverbs.

**Speaking**
Talking about holidays, interesting experiences.

**Listening**
Listening for gist.

**Reading**
Skimming.

**Learner training**
Strategies: listening for gist, skimming; practice in self-direction; activity evaluation.

## 1
### Your holiday

Work in a group. Show each other photos of your holiday or a place you visited recently and talk about it.

## 2
### Interesting experiences

Below are four holiday photos. Listen to Bill, Annette and Marti talking about what they did on holiday. As you listen, write the names of the people who took the photos and where they took them. Which photo didn't they take?

Compare answers with other people in the class.

a) Name: _____    Place: _____

b) Name: _____    Place: _____

c) Name: _____    Place: _____

d) Name: _____    Place: _____

Listen again and note down the key words which helped you to understand.

How well did you understand? Discuss any problems you had.

# 3
## Anne's travel diary

Read this extract from Anne's travel diary. Where did she have her holiday?

Monday, 1st July

At last we arrived at the reef. The sun shone brightly and a cool wind blew quite strongly from the ocean. I changed into my swimsuit and got ready. I was so excited! In front of me the reef showed darkly under the blue water and I could see brown bits of coral above the water here and there. The water was so cold! I gasped as I lowered myself slowly from the boat into the dark water. I adjusted my mask and took a quick look under the water. The scene below was incredible! There were mountains, valleys and forests of corals and colourful fish. The current wasn't strong, so I snorkelled excitedly for half an hour and didn't notice the cold water. I watched bright parrot fish feed happily on the coral, shoals of large red fish swim harmlessly past and, at one point, saw an enormous sea wrasse, about two metres long, which moved fast when it saw me. It was quite harmless. I didn't want to get out of the water at all! The Great Barrier Reef was a great experience.

How much did you understand? 20 per cent, 30 per cent, more? How much do you need to understand to answer the question?

# 4
## It's your choice! (1)

Choose one of these two activities.

### a) Vocabulary

Read Anne's travel diary again and make a list of words you don't know but think are important. Find out their meanings. Can you explain them in English?

### b) Grammar

Read Anne's travel diary again and make a list of any verbs in the simple past you don't know. Find out their meanings and present tense forms. Add them to your verb bank.

Feedback: Present your findings to the class.

# 5
## Grammar check

Work with a partner or in a group. Look at the differences between these two sentences:

a) I was excited.

b) I snorkelled excitedly.

Find more adjectives and adverbs in Anne's travel diary. How are adverbs formed? How are they used?

### Activate your grammar
#### Adjectives and adverbs

| Adjectives | Adverbs |
| --- | --- |
| excited | excitedly |
| quick | quickly |
| careful | carefully |
| happy | happily |
| fast | fast |

➡ See Grammar Review 13 on page 77.

# 6
## It's your choice! (2)

**With a partner or group**

Talk about an interesting experience you had on holiday. Show photos if you have some.

**On your own**

Write about an interesting experience you had on holiday or on some other occasion.

# 7
## Feedback

Say what you thought about some of the activities in this unit. Complete these sentences:

**Activity** _____ **was/wasn't interesting because** _____

_____

_____

**Activity** _____ **was/wasn't useful because** _____

_____

_____

**My favourite activity was** _____ **because** _____

_____

_____

**In Self-study**
**Workbook Unit 9**
Reading comprehension; practice in adjectives and adverbs; focus on sequencers.

## Grammar
Further practice in the simple past: modal verbs, irregular verbs.

## Reading
Skimming.

## Vocabulary
Word-building: prefixes.

## Learner training
Practice in self-direction; language awareness: word-building; strategies for guessing unknown words; strategies for reading newspaper articles; exploring reading interests; self-assessment.

# In the press

# 10

# 1

## In the news

What's in the news this week? Work in a group and talk about the stories you found interesting.

# 2

## From the newspapers

Look at the headlines. What do you think the stories are about?

Skim the stories and match these headlines to the stories.

a) **FLIGHT OF A LIFETIME!**

b) Dangerous Dog

c) WOMAN FALLS 3,000 FT AND LIVES!

## Activate your grammar

**Simple past: modal verbs**

| Present | Simple past |
|---|---|
| can | could |
| cannot/can't | could not/couldn't |
| must | had to |
| (have to) | (had to) |

➡ **See Grammar Review 14 on page 77.**

---

**1**

A poodle called Shona caused the deaths of three people in Sydney last week. The dog fell from a 13th floor balcony and killed Jenny Glade when it landed on her head.

As people gathered around her body, a bus knocked down an onlooker, Susan Batty, and killed her. Then another onlooker, Fred Smart, who couldn't take the shock, had a heart attack and died in an ambulance on the way to hospital.

*Daily News* **1st April 1996**

---

**2**

Ms Sarah Grant, 24, nearly died when her parachute failed to open during a sky-dive yesterday. She tried her emergency parachute, but that didn't open either. 'I was terrified. I expected to die,' she said afterwards from her hospital bed.

Sarah was lucky. She had a soft landing in some trees. She broke her left hip, both arms and three ribs, but is happy to be alive. 'I couldn't believe it when I found I was still alive!' she told reporters yesterday.

*The Star* 1/4/96

---

**3**

On Saturday, Pee Wee Kludd, 53, a sausage maker from Selby, S. Dakota, attached more than 40 helium-filled balloons to an aluminum deckchair and strapped himself in.

His unusual craft took off from his garden and reached a height of nearly 2,000 ft over the town.

After 90 minutes, he decided to return to earth. To do this, he had to shoot 10 of the balloons. He then floated slowly down for a soft landing.

He said afterwards, 'It was wonderful. My life's ambition.'

**The Chronicle, 4.1.1996**

# 3
## Guess the meaning

a) Did you understand these words? If not, can you guess their meanings?

onlooker    craft    heart attack

parachute    floated

How did you guess the meanings?

b) Look at the stories again and underline words you don't understand.

Are these words important to understand the story? Are they important for you to learn?

Can you guess their meanings?

### Learning tip
**How to guess the meanings of new words**

**Try this. Ask yourself:**

1 Do I understand the general topic of
  a) the text?
  b) the paragraph?
  c) the sentence?

2 Does it look like a word I know
  a) in English?
  b) in another language?

3 Do I know part of the word? Prefix? Suffix?

4 What kind of word is it? Verb? Adjective?

5 What does the word sound like?

What can you say about the words around the question mark below?

Compare ideas with a partner. Why is guessing an unknown word a useful strategy when reading?

# 4
## It's your choice! (1)
### Word-building

Use a dictionary to find six more words that you want to learn that begin with one of the following prefixes:

a) un-      b) dis-      c) re-

What do your words mean? Write a sentence for each word.

Present your findings to the class. What do the prefixes 'un-', 'dis-' and 're-' mean?

# 5
## It's your choice! (2)
**Reading the press**

Work on your own or with a partner. Choose an English language newspaper or magazine and find an interesting story to read and work on.

When you are ready, tell someone else about the story and why you found it interesting.

Feedback: Did you learn anything new? If so, what? Was your story easy or difficult to understand? Why?

## Learning tip
**Reading a newspaper or magazine story**

**Before you read:**

a) Look at the headline.
b) Look at the pictures.

**What is the topic of the story?**

**While you read:**

a) Skim (read quickly to get the main ideas).
b) Don't worry about new words.
c) Read again if you want to.

**Try to guess the meanings of new words.**

# 6
## Feedback

How well did you do in this unit? Tick (✓) your answers and say why.

| Activity | I did very well | I did OK | I didn't do very well | Why? |
|---|---|---|---|---|
| 1 | | | | |
| 2 | | | | |
| 3a | | | | |
| 3b | | | | |
| 4 | | | | |
| 5 | | | | |

**In Self-study Workbook Unit 10**
Practice in guessing the meanings of words; 'have to', 'must', 'can'; listening comprehension; how to listen to the news.

## A
### Progress check

Do these activities to check your progress.

### 1 Mayumi Obe, personal assistant

Mayumi Obe has a busy and responsible job; she is the personal assistant of Helen Webster, the director of a large advertising agency in Tokyo.

Look at the sentences below and then listen to Mayumi talking about her work routine. Write 'T' or 'F' to show which sentences are true and which are false.

|  | true/false |
|---|---|
| a) Mayumi often starts work at 7 am. |  |
| b) Helen generally comes in after 9 am. |  |
| c) Mayumi always checks Helen's diary first. |  |
| d) Helen usually makes her own coffee. |  |
| e) Helen sometimes dictates letters to Mayumi for two hours. |  |
| f) Mayumi always checks the post. |  |
| g) Most of the post is for Helen. |  |
| h) Mayumi sometimes checks the newspapers for interesting articles. |  |
| i) Mayumi occasionally visits new clients with Helen. |  |
| j) Mayumi never goes on business trips abroad with Helen. |  |
| k) Mayumi usually eats lunch at her desk. |  |
| l) Mayumi never leaves work before 6.30. |  |

*Check your answers from the Answer Key. Give yourself 1 point for each correct answer.*

### 2 Diary

Write about six things you did or didn't do yesterday.

Give your writing to a partner to check; check your partner's writing.

*Start with 25 points. Take off 1 point for every mistake. Add up to 15 points for length and detail. Discuss your score.*

### 3 Detective

Work with a partner. You are detectives working on a murder case. Read this statement by the victim's husband. Make a list of questions you want to ask him when you interview him again.

I arrived home from work at the usual time, 8 o'clock. The house was quiet and my wife didn't answer when I called her. I thought she was out. I was in a hurry to go out to meet a business client, so I went to the bathroom for a shower. When I went into the bedroom afterwards to get dressed, I found a note on the bedside table. It said, 'You're a swine! Goodbye!'. I walked around the bed and then saw her body on the floor. There was a gun beside her. I think she killed herself.

*Give yourselves 5 points each for every question with no mistakes in it. Take off 1 point for every mistake.*

### Score

1 Mayumi Obe, personal assistant ☐

2 Diary ☐

3 Detective ☐

## 4 Adjectives and adverbs

Write a list of as many adjectives as you can remember in two minutes. Find a partner and exchange lists. Now write the adverbs next to the adjectives.

*Give yourself 1 point for each correct adjective you gave to your partner. Give yourself 1 point for each correct adverb you wrote on your partner's list. Check with your teacher or a dictionary if you are not sure if an adverb is correct.*

## 5 Time to talk

Work with a partner. Talk about what you did at the weekend or last week. Try to keep talking for one minute without pausing. Your partner should time you.

*Score 1 point for every second you talk. Add up to 10 bonus points for use of the simple past.*

## B
## Checklist

Use this checklist to record how you feel about your progress.

| I can | yes/no |
|---|---|
| talk about my routine and habits | |
| ask about other people's routines and habits | |
| say how often I do things | |
| talk about what I did and didn't do in the past | |
| ask about what other people did or didn't do in the past | |
| express dates and times | |
| apologise | |
| say where places are | |
| talk in English for at least one minute | |

| I know | yes/no |
|---|---|
| some ways to guess the meanings of new words | |
| about skimming and scanning | |
| some strategies for improving my listening | |
| about regular and irregular verbs in the simple past | |
| about adjectives and adverbs | |
| which learning activities I like | |
| some of my language learning problems | |

## C
## Personal plan

What problems do you have and how do you plan to help yourself?

**Problems**

**Plans**

**Grammar**
Question tags,
present progressive.

**Speaking**
Starting, holding
and finishing
social conversations.

**Listening**
Listening for gist;
listening for detail.

**Learner training**
Communication
strategies; improving
self-confidence; practice
in self-direction; activity
evaluation.

## 1
## How much English do you speak?

If you want to speak English well, you need to practise. However, it can be difficult to find someone to practise with outside the class.

a) Discuss the following questions with a partner or in a group.

Do you have the chance to speak to people in English?

If yes, who do you talk to?

How often do you talk to them?

What do you talk about?

b) We speak to people for two main reasons:

to get or give something (e.g. information, things, advice): in other words, to make a transaction;

to be friendly, to make contact: in other words, to socialise or to 'network'.

Which kind of conversation do you find the most difficult in English? Why?

## 2
## Networking

Carmen, a student in Brighton in the south of England, likes to network to practise her English. She spoke to four people in four different situations yesterday.

Listen to Carmen's conversations. Which four situations was Carmen in yesterday? Number the situations in the order you hear them.

Carmen and her neighbour

Carmen and a hair stylist

Carmen and her English friend's parent

Carmen and a cab driver

Carmen and a woman in a supermarket queue

Carmen and a woman with a baby

How well does Carmen know the person in each situation? How do you know?

## 4
## How to start a conversation

In an English-speaking country, you can start a conversation with someone by talking or asking about:

a) something neutral, such as the weather

b) something connected with the person, but not too personal, such as his/her garden, or what he/she is doing at the time

c) something personal, such as appearance or possessions (but what you say must be positive, not negative!)

🔊 Listen again to Carmen. How did she start her conversations?

### Activate your grammar
**Question tags**

It's a nice day, isn't it?
You aren't English, are you?
It hasn't rained for weeks, has it?
You don't come here often, do you?
The bus will be late again, won't it?

➡ See Grammar Review 15 on page 77.

**Present progressive: for actions in the present**

Are you going to the shops?
I'm going to my English class.
The queue isn't getting any shorter!
Is your husband feeling better?

➡ See Grammar Review 16 on page 77.

## 3
## Conversation topics

| pets | health | rent |
| the weather | money | appearance |
| work | family | |

In your country, what topics are OK to talk about with people you don't know very well?

Is it OK to talk about the same topics with English-speaking people you don't know very well?

# 5
## How to finish a conversation

a) How did Carmen and her conversation partners finish their conversations? How many other ways can you think of to finish a conversation politely?

b) How would you finish a conversation with someone you *didn't* want to talk to? Listen to Carmen talking to a man in a bar. What else could she say?

# 6
## Gambit!

Work in a group of three or four. Each person should write a brief description of someone to start a conversation with, as in the example on the right. (Other people in your group can help you.)

Now exchange papers with another group so that each person has a new piece of paper. Your teacher will explain the game.

Who:
I'm a handsome young man

Where:
Standing behind you in the canteen queue

Familiarity:
You haven't met me before

# 7
## It's your choice!

Choose one or more of the following activities that you think will be useful for you. You can work alone or with others if you prefer.

### Speaking

With a partner, take it in turns to roleplay different conversations. You don't know each other. One of you is from an English-speaking country. You are both:

a) in a cafe          c) in a cinema queue

b) at a bus stop      d) on a beach

For each situation, one partner should start the conversation and keep it going, and the other partner should try to finish the conversation.

Roleplay your best one for the class.

### Vocabulary

Start a personal phrase book for starting and holding conversations with people you don't know.

Decide on your categories or headings for each section (e.g. different topics, situations, polite starters).

Add a translation if you want to.

Tell the class about how you are organising your phrase book and give examples.

### Writing

Write the dialogue for a scene from a play between two people who know each other a little, but not very well. Set the scene and say who the people are.

Check your spelling and grammar.

Ask for comments and suggestions to improve your dialogue.

# 8
## Feedback

Answer the following questions:

a) What did you think of this unit? Why?

b) Do you think you will be able to socialise better in English now? Why?/ Why not?

c) What can you do to improve?

Discuss your answers.

In Self-study
**Workbook Unit 11**
Listening practice; focus on question tags: writing, intonation and listening.

**Grammar**
'Would like' + infinitive; 'what/how about' + gerund/noun; present progressive for future plans.

**Speaking**
Making, accepting and declining invitations; making suggestions.

**Listening**
Listening for gist; listening for detail.

**Reading**
Understanding formal invitations.

**Learner training**
Language awareness: register and formality; exploring attitudes and anxieties, building self-confidence; practice in self-direction; self-assessment.

# 1
## The first step

Making an invitation to someone you don't know very well can be quite nerve-racking in any language. Have you ever tried it in English? What happened? How did you feel? Discuss this with a partner.

Do you think it is acceptable for a woman to ask a man out? If yes, when and how? If no, why not?

# 2
## Being bold

GRAHAM AND DIANA MILLINGTON
REQUEST THE PLEASURE OF THE COMPANY OF

*Michael Hallam & partner*

FOR THEIR HOUSE-WARMING PARTY
ON SATURDAY, 27TH MARCH, 1993
8 PM TO 2 AM

AT
CARMEL LODGE
21 WEBSTER WALK
WALFORD
TELEPHONE 0171 427 1010

DRESS FORMAL

R.S.V.P.

Mike has received an invitation. Read it and answer the following questions:

a) Who is it from?
b) What kind of event is it?
c) What should he wear?
d) What should he take with him?
e) What does 'R.S.V.P.' mean?

Mike is divorced. He hasn't got a partner at the moment. He decides to invite Pat, a woman he has just met. She is also divorced and he thinks she is very attractive.

Listen to the conversation.
How does Mike feel? Why? Is he successful?

# 3
## How to invite someone

Work with a partner or in a group.

a) Listen again to Mike and Pat. What words did they use to give their invitations?

b) How many other ways can you think of?

c) Look at these examples of invitations. When could you use them?

1  **Fancy a quick cup of coffee, then?**

2  **Do you like Mozart? I've got tickets for a concert next week and I was wondering whether you might be interested in coming with me?**

Now tick invitation 1 or invitation 2 for each situation.

| Situation | 1 | 2 |
|---|---|---|
| A  You know the person quite well or very well. | | |
| B  You don't know the person well. | | |
| C  You feel very nervous. | | |
| D  It is important to you that the person accepts your invitation. | | |
| E  The invitation isn't particularly important to you. | | |
| F  You feel sure the person will accept your invitation. | | |
| G  You think the other person might not be interested in your invitation. | | |

d) What differences in language do you notice between invitation 1 and invitation 2?

e) Look at the list of examples you made in (b). Are your phrases very formal, medium formal or less formal? Discuss your ideas.

Choose the phrases you would be happy to use and practise saying them.

## Activate your grammar

| Structures with gerunds and nouns | Past progressive for invitations |
|---|---|
| How about          a swim? | I was wondering whether ... |
| What about         coming for a swim? | We were wondering if ... |
| Do you fancy | I was thinking you might like to ... |

➡ See Grammar Review 17 on page 78.   ➡ See Grammar Review 18 on page 78.

# 4
## Accepting and declining invitations

How did Pat decline Mike's invitation? What words did she use? How did she feel?

How did Mike accept Pat's invitation? What words did he use? How did he feel?

Listen to the cassette and practise saying the sentences.

# 5
## It's your choice!

Choose to work on one of the three topics below. (You may work alone or with someone else.)

**Yes**
Accepting an invitation

**No**
Declining an invitation

**Maybe**
Hesitating about an invitation

How many different ways can you think of to do this?

Present your suggestions to the class.

Which ones will you use? Practise saying them so that you sound convincing.

# 6
## Excuses, excuses

a) ... but I'm going to Amsterdam for the weekend.

b) I'm afraid I fell downstairs and hurt my leg and now I can't walk.

c) You see, I've promised to babysit for my neighbour – otherwise I'd love to!

Someone you really don't like very much has just invited you to a brass band concert on Saturday night. What excuse will you give when you decline?

Whose excuse is the best? Why?

### Activate your grammar
**Present progressive for future plans**

I'm going to Amsterdam this weekend.
We're flying to Paris on Monday.
I'm babysitting tonight.

➡ See Grammar Review 19 on page 78.

# 7
## The social whirl

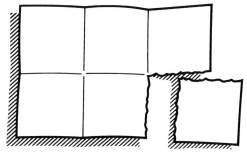

Take a sheet of blank paper and cut or tear it into six pieces.

Think of three invitations you would love to get (e.g. to watch a Cup Final at Wembley; to go to a party in Hollywood; to dine at the Ritz). Write them on three different pieces of paper.

Now think of three invitations you would hate to get (e.g. to go camping with your friends' children; to go fox hunting; to watch a Cup Final at Wembley). Write these on your other three pieces of paper.

Hand your papers to your teacher, who will tell you what to do next.

# 8
## Feedback

How well did you do in this unit? Tick (✓) your answers and give reasons.

| Activity | I did very well | I did OK | I didn't do very well | Why? |
|---|---|---|---|---|
| 1 | | | | |
| 2 | | | | |
| 3 | | | | |
| 4 | | | | |
| 5 | | | | |
| 6 | | | | |
| 7 | | | | |

# 13 Finding your way

**Grammar**
Imperatives; prepositions of location.

**Speaking**
Asking for, understanding and giving directions; getting someone's attention; thanking.

**Reading**
Reading for detail.

**Listening**
Listening for detail.

**Learner training**
Self-assessment; practice in self-direction; activity evaluation.

## Activity 1
## Tour of The Rocks

Mariko is having problems in Sydney. She is following the tour of The Rocks (the oldest part of Sydney) in her guidebook, but is lost. She marked her tour on her map. Where did she go wrong?

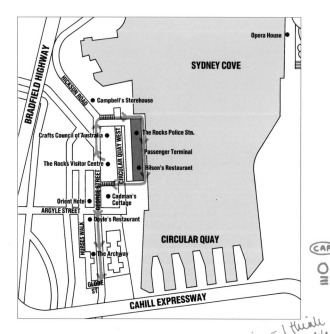

Tour 1: The Rocks

Begin at The Rocks Visitor Centre, where you can pick up information leaflets. Leave the Visitor Centre, go right past the Crafts Council of Australia and down Hickson Road. Go down the Customs Officers' Stairs by Campbell's Storehouse, an old warehouse built between 1838 and 1861. Cross to the waterside at the new Passenger Terminal and you will have a view across to Sydney opera House. Turn right and walk along the waterfront, passing the famous Doyle's and Bilson's restaurants, to the far end of the terminal. Go right again, across the road and up the stairs to the left of the Marionette Theatre. To the left of the stairs is Cadman's Cottage, Sydney's oldest house. At the top of the stairs turn left along George Street. Across the street are Unwins Stores (1844–46) and the Orient Hotel. On the other corner of Argyle Street is The Rocks Police Station. Just before the Fortune of War pub, turn right through the archway to reach Nurses Walk, then turn right again. This is the site of Australia's first hospital (1788–1916).

## Activity 2
## Listening

What should Mariko do? Listen to the cassette of Mariko and a passer-by. What did the passer-by tell her?

# 1
## Understanding directions

a) Here is a page of a new Australian English coursebook. The book is not finished – the publishers are checking it.

The book presents Mariko, a Japanese student, who is following her guidebook on a tour of The Rocks in Sydney.

The editor of the book has found a mistake on this page. You are Mike, the designer. Read 'Tour 1' in the book to find and correct the mistake in the map.

b) Now test Activity 1 in the book. Do the exercise yourself.

What do you think of the exercise? Why? What is its aim, do you think?

# 2
## Asking for directions

When you stop someone in the street to ask for help, you need to sound polite. How many of the following ways to stop someone could you use?

a) Hello! Hello!

b) Oi, you! Come here a minute!

c) Where's the station?

d) Where's the station, please?

e) Excuse me, where's the station, please?

f) Excuse me, I wonder if you could help me? I'm looking for the station.

g) Sorry to bother you, but I wonder if you could tell me how to get to the station from here?

Listen to the cassette and repeat.

Choose the expressions you would like to use. Practise saying them so you sound polite.

# 3
## Giving directions

On the book page in Exercise 1, there is an 'Activity 2' where Mariko asks a passer-by for directions. With a partner, write the cassette dialogue for Activity 2.

Act your scene for the class.

Now listen to the cassette recording made by the publisher of the book. What do you think of it? How does your scene compare?

Excuse Me!

### Activate your grammar
**Imperatives**

Turn right.
Turn left.
You turn right.
Keep going.
Go past ...
Take the first turning on the right.
Keep to the right-hand side.
Take the number 6 bus to ...

See Grammar Review 20 on page 78.

### Activate your language
**Prepositions of location**

It's on the right.          It's on the left.
It's to the right of ...    It's to the left of ...
It's opposite the station.
It's on the corner.
It's straight ahead.
It's near the park.
It's next to the supermarket.
It's in front of the hotel.
It's behind the cinema.

# 4
## It's your choice!

### Mystery tour: speaking or writing

Think of a well-known place or tourist sight that you know the way to from your school.

Tell or write the directions to someone else but don't say what the place is. Can your partner guess the place? Were your directions correct?

### Favourite places: speaking or writing

Where is your favourite restaurant? How do you get there?

Where is your favourite place for an evening out? How do you get there?

### Your place: speaking

Explain to someone how to get to your place from the school.

# 5
## Feedback

How well did you do in this unit?

| Skill | Self-assessment |
|---|---|
| **Understanding written directions** | |
| **Asking for directions politely** | |
| **Giving directions** | |
| **Responding to thanks** | |
| **Understanding spoken directions** | |

**In Self-study Workbook Unit 13**
Intonation practice for giving directions; reading comprehension with gap fill.

**Speaking**
Welcoming guests; offering, accepting and refusing things; asking for and giving permission; saying goodbye.

**Grammar**
'Must', 'have to' for obligation; 'may', 'could', 'can' for permission.

**Listening**
Listening for gist; listening for detail.

**Learner training**
Language awareness; practice in self-direction; activity evaluation; personal phrase book.

# Entertaining at home

# 14

# 1

## Other people's customs

Do you ever invite people to your home? If so, who?

How would you feel about guests doing the following?

Taking their shoes off at the door

Kissing you

Shaking your hand

Bringing you a gift of food or wine

Bringing you a gift of flowers

Bringing you nothing

Commenting on your home

Bringing small children

Arriving late

Arriving very late

Staying late

Leaving as soon as dinner is finished

Using your phone

Looking around your home

Not eating or drinking what you offer

What should you say and do if a guest from an English-speaking country brings you a gift?

# 2

## Ari and Stavros entertain

Ari and Stavros, two Greek students at Thames Valley University, have invited Jean and Cathie to their place for the evening.

 Listen to the cassette. How well do Jean and Cathie and Stavros and Ari know each other?

 Listen again. Are the following statements true or false?

a) Jean and Cathie have visited this flat before.

b) Jean and Cathie are late.

c) Stavros and Ari live near the river.

d) Jean has a glass of white wine.

e) Cathie has a glass of water.

f) Ari offers them retsina.

g) Ari offers them crisps.

h) Cathie asks permission to use the phone.

i) Ari agrees to let Cathie use the phone.

j) Jean asks permission to look at the bathroom.

k) Cathie asks permission to use the bedroom.

# 3
## How to be a good host

a) What can you say to welcome a guest to your home?

b) Look at the following ways of offering. Which could you use with:

your boss?
your daughter's boyfriend?
your best friend?

| | | |
|---|---|---|
| Would you like something to drink? | May I offer you something to drink? | Let me take your coat. |
| How about something to drink? | You must have something to drink. | I'll take your coat. |
| Drink? | | Give me your coat. |

### Activate your grammar
**'Must', 'have to', 'don't have to'**

| | |
|---|---|
| **You must try one of these cakes!** | **You don't have to eat it if you don't want to.** |
| **You must have some retsina.** | **You don't have to drink the retsina if you don't like it.** |
| **We must be going soon.** | **We don't have to be going yet.** |
| **He has to leave early.** | **He doesn't have to leave early.** |

➡ **See Grammar Review 21 on page 78.**

# 4
## How to ask for permission

Rank the following so that the most formal expression is numbered 1 and the least formal expression is numbered 5.

May I use your bathroom?

Could I use your toilet?

Where's the loo?

Can I use your toilet?

Do you mind if I use your toilet?

Do you know any other expressions for 'use the toilet'?

# 5
## How to be a perfect guest

📼 Listen to Stavros, Ari, Cathie and Jean having their dinner. What do Cathie and Jean say when Ari offers them more food? What else can you say?

# 6
## How to say goodbye

📼 What do you say when you want to leave? Listen to Cathie and Jean.

# 7
## Roleplays

Work in groups of four (two hosts and two guests). Take it in turns to play hosts and guests in these three situations.

The two hosts have invited the following guests for drinks or a meal at their home:

a) new neighbours

b) some students from their course

c) the senior partners in their company

Roleplay the first few minutes of the evening.

Roleplay the last few minutes of the evening.

# 8
## It's your choice!

### Speaking

Find a partner or partners and practise roleplaying hosts and guests. You can choose who the guests and hosts are and whether they have good or bad manners. Act out your best scene for the class.

### Writing

Write a scene for a play where Jean and Cathie invite Stavros and Ari to their flat for a meal.

# 9
## Feedback

Did you find the activities in this unit useful? Why?/Why not?

| Activities | Comments |
|---|---|
| 1 Other people's customs | |
| 2 Ari and Stavros entertain | |
| 3 How to be a good host | |
| 4 How to ask for permission | |
| 5 How to be a perfect guest | |
| 6 How to say goodbye | |
| 7 Roleplays | |
| 8 It's your choice! | |

**In Self-study**
**Workbook Unit 14**
Writing thank you notes; practice in offering, accepting and refusing; asking for and giving permission; thanking; giving compliments, 'must' and 'have to'; intonation practice.

# 15 Improve your telephone skills

**Speaking**
Making informal and formal telephone calls; leaving a message; intonation practice.

**Vocabulary**
Telephone-related language.

**Listening**
Listening for gist; listening for detail.

**Writing**
Handy Phone Phrase Cards; instructions.

**Learner training**
Building self-confidence; language awareness; practice in self-direction; self-assessment.

## 1
### How do you feel?

How often do you speak in English on the telephone?

Who do you speak to on the phone?

How do you feel about making calls in English? Why?

Do you have any problems? What?

## 2
### Vocabulary

How many different expressions do you know for telephoning? E.g.:

to telephone
to call

## 3
### Telephone quiz

When you telephone in English, there are certain expressions which are usually used. Do you know them?

Work with a partner to choose the best answers in the telephone quiz below. Sometimes more than one answer is possible.

1. You call your friend, John. When he picks up the phone, you should say:
   a. Hello!
   b. Hello, I'm (your name).
   c. Hello, this is (your name) here.

2. You're not sure if it is John answering the phone. You should ask:
   a. Are you John?
   b. John?
   c. Is that John?

3. It isn't John. It's his father. You should ask:
   a. Where's John?
   b. Give me John, please.
   c. Could I speak to John, please?
   d. I'd like to speak to John, please.
   e. Is John there, please?

4. You want to ask someone on the phone to wait while you find a pen to write something down. You should say:
   a. Wait, please.
   b. One moment.
   c. Hold on, please.
   d. Just a moment.

5. The person you want to speak to isn't there. You should say:
   a. I'll call back later.
   b. I call later.

6. You want to leave a message. You should say:
   a. Tell him to meet me at 8 pm tomorrow.
   b. Here is a message. Meet me at 8 pm tomorrow.
   c. Could I leave a message, please?
   d. Could you give him a message, please?

Discuss your answers with your partner.

Now listen to Jean and Stavros on the phone to check your answers. Do you know any other telephone expressions?

# 4
## Who is Nina?

 Listen to Jean and Ari.

a) Who is Nina?

b) How does Jean feel?

c) What does Ari say when he can't hear or understand Jean?

d) What else could you say in that situation?

# 5
## Formal phoning

When you talk to someone you don't know on the phone (for example, when you make a business call), you need to know more formal telephone expressions.

Listen to Ari making a phone call. What is the situation? Why is he making this call?

Listen again and note down any expressions you hear that you think would be useful to know when making a formal phone call.

Do you know any others?

# 6
## Finishing a call

There are many expressions you can use to finish a phone call, but it is important that you use the right intonation – or you might sound unfriendly.

Listen again to the endings of the three telephone conversations: first, Jean and Stavros, then Jean and Ari, finally Ari and the hotel reservations clerk.

Listen to the cassette and practise saying the expressions under 'Activate your language' in a friendly or polite way.

### Activate your language
**Finishing a phone call**

OK. Bye!
See you!
Take care!
Thanks for calling. Bye!
Thank you. Goodbye!

# 7
## Telephone game

Work with a partner. Take it in turns to make and answer calls. Sit back to back so you can't see each other's faces.

**Partner A**
From the list, choose three **people** to call. You need to speak to them urgently.

**Partner B**
Answer as the receptionist at any of the **companies** from the list. You can either say the person is not there (and take a message), or play the role of that person too.

Act out your best roleplay for the class.

| People |
| --- |
| Philip Sinclair |
| Kim Green |
| Peter Lugg |
| Judith Lindley |
| The Director |
| Annie Park |
| Paul Doyle |

| Companies |
| --- |
| Dynamo Sports Equipment Ltd |
| Gretton Displays PLC |
| Jennison, Whitney & Co. Ltd |
| Scottish Pride Cakes Ltd |
| Wallace Ltd |
| Travel Insurance Services |
| Crackpot Computers Ltd |

# 8
## It's your choice!

**Speaking**
Go out of the class and make a real phone call in English. Your teacher will give you a number to call.

**Speaking**
Use a cassette recorder to practise leaving recorded messages on an answering machine.

To leave a message:

1 Say who you are.
2 Say the date and the time of your call.
3 Leave your message.

Call:

a) your friend, Bill, to tell him where and when to meet you tonight

b) your brother, to discuss your mother's operation

c) an old school friend you haven't seen for 10 years

**Reading/writing**
Write instructions in English for using a public phone. Use a dictionary to help you.

**Learning tip**

Make a handy Phone Phrase Card to keep by your telephone to help you remember key expressions. Discuss your choice with someone else.

# 9
## Feedback

How well did you do in this unit?

| Activity | Self-assessment |
| --- | --- |
| 2  Vocabulary | |
| 3  Telephone quiz | |
| 4  Who is Nina? | |
| 5  Formal phoning | |
| 6  Finishing a call | |
| 7  Telephone game | |
| 8  It's your choice! | |

**In Self-study Workbook Unit 15**
Telephoning and note-taking; listening self-assessment; telephone manners; reading self-assessment.

# REVIEW 3

## Score

1 Who's talking?

2 Starting a
  conversation

3 Invitations

4 Excuses

5 Directions

## A

### Progress check

Do these activities to check
your progress.

### 1 Who's talking?

Listen to the conversation.
Who's talking? Tick the correct
answer below.

a) Carmen and a stranger

b) Carmen and a close friend

c) Carmen and a person she
   knows a little

*Check your answers from the Answer
Key. Give yourself 10 points for a
correct answer.*

### 2 Starting a conversation

You are on a coach trip to
Margate. An attractive person you
have never met is sitting next to
you. How many different opening
lines can you think of for a
conversation with this person?
Write them down. You have
three minutes.

*Give your list to someone else to
check. Check someone else's list.
Start with 10 points for each
opening line. Take off 1 point for
each grammar or spelling mistake.
Take off 2 points if the language
is not appropriate.*

### 3 Invitations

Invite the following people to the
events listed below. Write down
what you would say.

| People | Events |
|---|---|
| a) Your sister | To go shopping with you |
| b) Your boss | To dinner at your place |
| c) Your teacher | To go for a coffee with you |

*Give your writing to someone else to
check. Check someone else's writing.
Start with 10 points for each
invitation. Take off 1 point for each
grammar or spelling mistake. Add
up to 2 points to each for appropriate
use of language. Discuss and agree
your scores.*

### 4 Excuses

Your sister, your boss and your
teacher decline your invitations.
Write what they say.

*Give your writing to someone else to
check. Check someone else's writing.
Start with 5 points for each answer.
Take off 1 point for each grammar or
spelling mistake. Add up to 2 points
to each for appropriate use of
language. Add up to 5 points to each
for a good excuse. Discuss and agree
your scores.*

### 5 Directions

Write the
directions for
getting from
Palace Pier
to the Theatre
Royal, using
the map of
Brighton below.

*Start with 25
points. Take off
1 point for every
mistake. Add
up to 25 points
for detail.*

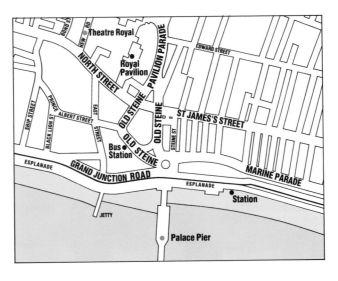

## 6 Asking permission

Work with a partner. One of you should ask permission in (a) and the other in (b).

a) Ask a passer-by on the street if you can use his portable telephone to make an urgent call.

b) Ask a senior colleague hosting a dinner party at her house if you can use her toilet.

*You should give your partner a score. Give up to 30 points for being polite and using the appropriate language. Check with the suggested answers in the Answer Key. Discuss and agree on the scores.*

## 7 Telephoning

Work with a partner. One of you should make a call in (a) and the other in (b). The person you want to speak to isn't there, so you should leave a message.

a) Call a new business contact, Ann Short. You want to ask her to lunch on Monday to meet your boss.

b) Call your personal accountant, Adrian Jones. You want to ask if he can tell you how much tax you have to pay.

*You should give your partner a score for both making and answering the calls. Give up to a total of 60 points. Discuss and agree on your scores.*

## B

### Checklist

Use this checklist to record how you feel about your progress.

| I can | yes/no | I know | yes/no |
|---|---|---|---|
| start up and hold a social conversation | | what topics to talk about in social conversations | |
| invite someone to do something | | some differences between formal and informal speech | |
| accept or decline an invitation | | | |
| understand and give directions | | some telephone expressions used in English | |
| ask permission to do something | | about question tags | |
| give and refuse permission | | | |
| offer things or to do something | | intonation for sounding polite | |
| accept and refuse an offer | | which learning activities I like | |
| make telephone calls | | some of my learning problems | |

## C

### Personal plan

What problems do you have and how do you plan to help yourself?

**Problems**

**Plans**

**Now add up your total score**

200-270 Brilliant!
150-199 Very good.
100-149 Satisfactory. Don't forget to review the units regularly.
0-99 You need to review Units 11-15 again.

| Grammar | Listening | At the deli |
| Count and mass nouns; word-building: adjectives; comparatives. | Listening for specific information. | |

**Speaking**
Talking about food: appearance, smell, taste, feel.

**Learner training**
Practice in self-direction; vocabulary learning strategy: grouping; activity evaluation.

# 16

## 1
### Memorable meals

What's the best meal you've ever eaten? What's the worst meal you've ever eaten?

## 2
### Picnic

a)  What food would you take to a picnic party on the beach? Discuss this in a group.

b)  Listen to Chris and Alan discussing what to take to a picnic. In the list below, circle the items they plan to take.

| | | |
|---|---|---|
| apple juice | duck paté | quiche |
| avocado | grapes | rolls |
| bacon | ham | sausage |
| bread | lettuce | stuffed olives |
| cake | mineral water | tomato |
| cheese | orange juice | tuna |
| chocolate | pancake | |

c)  Put the listed words into groups. Use any categories you like. Find three more words for each group. Use a dictionary to help you.

Show your groups to a partner and ask him/her to guess what your categories are.

### Learning tip

**Grouping new words can help you remember them.**

## 3
### Count and mass nouns

a)  Work with a partner. Look at the examples in the table below. What differences can you see between count and mass nouns?

| Count nouns: examples | Mass nouns: examples |
|---|---|
| an egg, two rolls, half a dozen bananas, twenty olives | Wine, bread, cheese, butter, milk |
| I'd like a banana.<br>I'd like some olives.<br>These olives taste good. | I'd like some cheese.<br>This cheese tastes good. |
| A: How many rolls should we take?<br>B: Six. | A: How much wine should we take?<br>B: Two bottles. |

b) Which of the words in the list in Exercise 2 are count nouns and which are mass nouns?

### Activate your grammar
**Count and mass nouns**

| Count nouns | Mass nouns |
|---|---|
| **an egg** | **milk** |
| **a potato** | **honey** |
| **crisps** | **bread** |

 **See Grammar Review 22 on page 79.**

# 4
## How much would you like?

Brainstorm! Add different types of food to complete the phrases below in as many ways as possible. How many more phrases like these do you know?

a slice of      a piece of      a bit of

# 5
## Chris and Alan at the deli

Listen to Chris and Alan discussing the food in the delicatessen.

a) What was the problem with the goat's cheese?

b) What was the problem with the camembert?

c) Which cheese did they buy? Why? How much?

d) What was the problem with the avocados?

e) Which grapes did they buy? Why? How many?

Listen to more expressions describing food using 'too' and 'enough'. Practise saying them.

**Activate your grammar**

**'Too' and 'not enough'**

Chocolate is too sweet for me.
Indian food is too hot for me.

Chinese food isn't spicy enough for me.
Strawberries without sugar aren't sweet
  enough for me.

➡ See Grammar Review 23 on page 79.

**Comparatives: '-er', 'less than', 'more than', 'as … as'**

This bread roll is fresher than that one.
These grapes are sweeter than those ones.
These olives are softer than those ones.
This cheese is creamier than that one.

This cheese is less creamy than that one.
This pizza is more delicious than that one.
These grapes aren't as tasty as those ones.

➡ See Grammar Review 24 on page 79.

# 6

## Describing food

Below are some words for describing food. Which words describe the way food
a) looks? b) feels? c) smells?
d) tastes?

Do you know any other words for describing food?

### Activate your grammar
**Word-building: adjectives**

| Noun | Adjective |
|------|-----------|
| salt | salty |
| butter | buttery |
| cream | creamy |
| spice | spicy |
| garlic | garlicky |
| chocolate | chocolaty |
| fish | fishy |
| oil | oily |

# 7

## Discussing food

Work with a partner. Compare your opinions about these foods:

vanilla ice-cream and chocolate ice-cream

bananas and grapefruit

chilli sauce and tomato ketchup

Talk about foods you don't like to eat and say why.

# 8

## It's your choice!

Choose the activity you think will be the most useful or the most enjoyable for you. Work alone or with others. Use a dictionary to help you and make a note of any new words you want to remember.

**Speaking or writing**

Describe your favourite food. Why do you like it?

**Speaking or writing**

Describe the typical food you eat for a special occasion or holiday in your country or another country you know.

**Discussion**

Plan a class picnic or party. What food and drink do you need? How much?

**Writing**

Start a food diary. Write in it what you ate yesterday, what it was like, if you enjoyed it and why.

# 9

## Feedback

What did you think about the activities in this unit?

| Activity | Comments |
|----------|----------|
| 1  Memorable meals | |
| 2  Picnic | |
| 3  Count and mass nouns | |
| 4  How much would you like? | |
| 5  Chris and Alan at the deli | |
| 6  Describing food | |
| 7  Discussing food | |
| 8  It's your choice! | |

**In Self-study**
**Workbook Unit 16**
Reading comprehension: comparing food; 'too ...', 'not ... enough'; count and mass nouns.

# 17 Eating out

## 1
### Eating out

Work in a group and discuss the following questions:

a) When did you last eat out? Where? What did you eat? Did you enjoy it? Who paid the bill?

b) What about paying a restaurant bill in your country? Can each person pay separately? Are men expected to pay the bill? Is it necessary to tip? How much?

## 2
### Hungry?

a) Imagine you are going out for a meal after this class. What do you fancy eating?

Look at the three menus. Which restaurant would you choose?

1

## Newbery's

**SOUPS AND STARTERS**
French Onion Soup
Baked Artichokes
Avocado and Lime Salad
Pancake with Caviare
Braised Lamb's Brains

**FISH**
Lobster Thermidor
Fresh Trout

**MEAT**
Lamb Kebabs
Pork with Lemon
Veal with Orange
Steak
Chicken Hotpot

**VEGETABLES**
French Beans
Sweet Baby Carrots
Garden Peas
New English Potatoes
Pommes Frites
Curried Vegetables
Steamed White Rice

**SALADS**
Fresh Green Salad
Chef's Salad
Tomato Salad

2

 # Big Buns

**starters**
- Crispy Nachos with hot, melted cheese £2.50
- Stuffed Green Peppers £3.50
- Shrimp Gumbo Soup £3.00
- Cowpoke Special with baked beans £2.50

**burgers**
- Quarter Pounder £5.00
- Quarter Pounder with melted cheese £5.45
- Beef, Bacon, Lettuce & Tomato Special £6.00
- Home on the Range £6.75
  double beef burger, fried beans, chilli sauce & melted cheese
- Lonesome Cowboy £4.50
  burger with fried egg
- Aloha Burger £5.50
  pineapple and ham

▶ **All burgers served with side salad, coleslaw and French fries.**

## Hong Kong
### Chinese restaurant

**Cantonese Style**

| | | |
|---|---|---|
| 1 | Crispy Duck | £5.80 |
| 2 | Crispy Beef with Hot Sauce | £4.80 |
| 3 | Singapore Rice Noodle | £4.30 |
| 4 | Roast Duck and Pineapple | £4.50 |
| 5 | Lemon Chicken with Sauce | £3.80 |
| 6 | Roast Pork Chinese Style | £3.80 |
| 7 | Roast Duck Chow Mein | £4.50 |
| 8 | King Prawns | £4.50 |

**Soup**

| | | |
|---|---|---|
| 9 | Hong Kong Special Soup | £1.50 |
| 10 | Sweet Corn with Chicken | £1.50 |
| 11 | Crab Meat and Sweet Corn | £2.00 |
| 12 | Won Ton Soup | £2.00 |

**Rice**

| | | |
|---|---|---|
| 13 | Special Fried Rice | £2.90 |
| 14 | King Prawn Fried Rice | £3.20 |
| 15 | Chicken Fried Rice | £2.80 |
| 16 | Fried Rice with Egg | £1.60 |
| 17 | Plain Boiled Rice | £1.50 |

**Sweet & Sour**

| | | |
|---|---|---|
| 18 | Sweet & Sour Chicken | £2.90 |
| 19 | Sweet & Sour Prawns | £3.90 |
| 20 | Sweet & Sour Pork | £2.90 |

b) When you looked at the menus, did you:

| | | | |
|---|---|---|---|
| read them quickly (skim them) to get a general idea of the type of food on each of the menus? | look quickly for the type of food you wanted to eat (scan them) and then read the parts that interested you? | read them carefully because you weren't sure what you wanted to eat? | read them carefully in case there were words you didn't know? |

c) The way you read a menu (or any other text) is affected by your reason for reading it.

How would you 'read' a telephone directory? Why?

How would you read a recipe? Why?

## 3

### At a restaurant

a) Listen to the cassette. Which restaurant from Exercise 2 did Sandra and Pete go to?

b) What did they order? Tick the items on the menu.

### Activate your language
**Ordering in a restaurant**

I'd like the soup, please.
I'll have the artichokes, please.
I'll go for the chicken hotpot.

## 4

### It's your choice!
**Roleplay**

Work in groups of three or four. One of you has invited the others for a meal in one of the restaurants in Exercise 2. Decide which restaurant to visit and discuss what you want to eat from the menu.

## 5

### Are you a vegetarian?

'Not exactly. I don't eat any meat at all, but I do eat some fish. I don't eat some seafood because I'm allergic to it.'
*Linda, Windsor*

'I eat some meat; mutton and chicken, mostly. I don't eat any pork because I'm Muslim.'
*Rosli, Brunei*

'I don't eat any animal products at all. I don't eat any meat, dairy food, eggs or fish. I'm a vegan.'
*Peter, Auckland*

Is there anything you don't eat? Why not? Discuss this with a partner.

# 6
## Some and any

a) Work with a partner or in a group. Look at Linda's, Halimah's and Peter's statements in Exercise 5 and the 'Activate your grammar' examples below. What is the difference between 'some' and 'any'? Discuss your ideas.

b) Write some sentences about what you eat, using 'some', 'any', 'something' and 'anything'.

### Activate your grammar
**'Some/any'; 'something/anything'**

I don't like some seafood.
I like any food with garlic in it.
Have you got some strawberries?
Have they got any Chinese tea?
I don't eat anything with with meat in it.
I'd like something sweet for dessert.

➡ See Grammar Review 25 on page 79.

# 7
## The most delicious food in town

Discuss these questions with a partner or in a group.

a) What was the most expensive meal you have ever eaten? Describe it. Was it worth the money?

b) What was the most delicious dessert you have ever eaten? Why?

c) What was the spiciest or hottest meal you have ever eaten? Where did you eat it?

d) Where can you get the tastiest pizzas in this area?

e) Which restaurant has the most mouth-watering menu you know of? Describe it.

Think of two more questions to ask your partner about food.

### Activate your grammar
**Superlatives**

the hottest meal
the spiciest food
the most expensive meal
the most delicious pizza
the best restaurant
the worst dessert

➡ See Grammar Review 26 on page 79.

# 8
## It's your choice!

Choose the activity you think will be most useful or interesting.

### Discussion

You are opening a new restaurant in the area. Decide:

what kind of restaurant it is

who your typical customers are

your menu

Use a dictionary to help you and make a note of any new words you want to remember.

### Grammar notes

Make a list of adjectives and find out their comparative and superlative forms. For example:

| Adjective | Comparative | Superlative |
|---|---|---|
| hot | hotter | hottest |
| delicious | more delicious | most delicious |

Look at the words in Exercise 6, Unit 16. Use a grammar reference book to help you.

# 9
## Feedback

What did you learn from this unit?

_____

What do you need to do more work on?

_____

**In Self-study**
**Workbook Unit 17**
Reading comprehension: recipe; more practice in 'something' and 'anything', comparatives and superlatives.

# 1
## Have you ever ...?

Have you ever:

a) lost your car keys?

b) forgotten your partner's birthday?

c) forgotten where you parked the car?

d) been sick in public?

e) lost your passport while abroad?

f) left your coat in a restaurant?

g) fallen off a bicycle?

h) lost a wallet or purse?

i) missed your flight?

j) lost your job?

k) fallen downstairs?

l) broken someone's expensive vase?

**Answers**

Yes, I have.

No, I haven't.

No, never.

Think of one more question to ask a partner.

Talk about one thing that has happened to you. When did it happen? What did you do?

**Activate your grammar**
**Present perfect: questions**

**Have you ever eaten lobster?**
**Has she ever missed an appointment?**
**Have you already met my partner?**

See Grammar Review 27 on page 80.

# 2
## You'll never guess what's happened!

a) Listen to the speakers on the cassette. Which of the things in Exercise 1 have just happened to them? Tick (✓) these things on the list.

b) How did their partners react?

**Activate your language**
**Reacting to bad news**

**Oh dear!**
**Poor you!**
**What? Surely not!**
**How terrible!**

# 3
## It's your choice!

Choose either activity (a) or activity (b) to find out more about the present perfect. You can work alone or with someone else.

If you like discussing things, analysing information and working things out for yourself, you might like to choose activity (a). If you enjoy looking things up, researching and working with books, you might like to choose activity (b).

### Activity (a)

Both the present perfect and the simple past are used when we talk about the past. However, there are differences in use and meaning, as well as form.

Compare the present perfect sentences with the simple past sentences in the table below: what differences can you see?

Present your ideas to the class on an OHT or on the board.

### Activity (b)

Work with two or three different grammar reference books for learners of English. Look up the present perfect and find out about its form, its meanings and how it is used. Compare what the different books say.

Prepare an A4 sized 'fact sheet' on the present perfect which can be copied and given to each member of the class. Put on it anything you think is useful.

| Present perfect | Simple past |
|---|---|
| You'll never guess what's happened! | You'll never guess what happened next! |
| I've lost my job. | I lost my job last month. |
| What have you done? | What did you do when it happened? |
| I've lost my passport. | I lost my passport while we were on holiday. |
| Have you seen it today? | Did you see it yesterday? |
| Maybe you've left it in the Ladies. | Maybe you left it in the Ladies at lunch time. |
| I've missed my flight! | I missed my flight this morning. |
| I've booked a room in the airport hotel. | I booked a room in the airport hotel last night. |
| I've managed to get a seat on a flight tomorrow. | I managed to get a seat on a flight the next day. |
| I've booked theatre tickets for tomorrow night. | I booked theatre tickets for the next night. |

# 4
## Test yourself

Learners of English often make mistakes using tenses. Some of the following sentences contain mistakes. Which ones? Can you correct them?

a) I have seen this film last week.

b) Have you ever been to France?

c) He's cleaned the car this morning.

d) We've just put the children to bed.

e) Oh dear! I was just sick.

f) They lived in Birmingham for six years.

g) They have lived in Birmingham for six years.

Discuss your answers.

# 5
## A long time

I've been a vegetarian for ten years.

I've lived in Walnut Creek since 1957.

Write more sentences for each of these patterns.

# 6
## Your greatest achievements

*'I've lost 25 kilos! It's taken me two years.'*
*Pearson Brown,*
*Tobago, West Indies*

*'I've qualified as a marine engineer!'*
*Louise Finlay,*
*Aberdeen, Scotland*

*'I've brought up two children on my own.'*
*Jo Grummet,*
*Napier, New Zealand*

*'I've written a book about my life.'*
*Bill Rockingham,*
*Southampton, England*

In a group of four or five, talk about your own personal achievements.

# 7
## Feedback

What have you learnt in this unit?

_____

_____

What have you practised?

_____

_____

**Pearson Brown**

**Louise Finlay**

**Jo Grummet**

**Bill Rockingham**

**In Self-study**
**Workbook Unit 18**
Vocabulary learning quiz;
reacting to bad news:
intonation practice;
listening practice.

# 19 Taking control

**Grammar**
Recycling of simple past, present perfect; past progressive; imperatives.

**Speaking**
Leaving messages on an answering machine; discussion; asking for repetition, clarification, spelling.

**Listening**
Listening for specific information.

**Learner training**
Strategies for taking control of a conversation; building confidence in using the telephone; practice in self-direction; self-assessment.

## 1
### Meeting new people

What advice would you give to someone who is lonely and wants to meet new people?

## 2
### Making contact

a) Martin is looking for a new relationship. He has advertised in the 'lonely hearts' section of his local newspaper.

> **Attractive, unattached male, 37**, non-smoker, own home, interested in travel, cinema, motorbikes & 60s rock music, seeks woman for nights out, holidays, friendship and maybe more. A partner for life? Box no. 333566

He received letters from 23 women who saw his ad in the paper. He thought two of them looked interesting and decided to phone them.

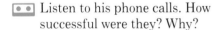 Listen to his phone calls. How successful were they? Why?

b) Do you think this is a good way to meet partners? Why? / Why not? Is this usual in your country? Why? / Why not?

### Activate your grammar
**Past progressive**

**I was looking through the replies and I liked your letter a lot.**
**He was looking at a newspaper when she saw him.**
**We were eating dinner when the phone rang.**

 **See Grammar Review 28 on page 80.**

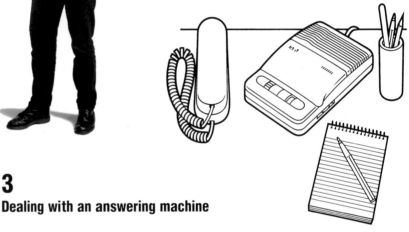

## 3
### Dealing with an answering machine

a) Leaving a message on an answering machine can be stressful. Work with a partner or in a group and discuss what tips you would give about how to deal with an answering machine; for example:

Always practise saying your message in advance.

Make a list. Compare your ideas.

b) Work with a partner. Imagine you are on your way to meet the following people, but something has made you late. Take it in turns to call them and leave a message on their answering machines. (Use a cassette recorder, if possible.)

Colin Harrison, your tax adviser

a classmate

Ann Heron, your psychotherapist

## Learning tip

Understanding someone on the phone can be difficult. Sometimes you can miss important information or have problems taking part in the conversation. It is a good idea to have some strategies for taking control of the conversation whenever you have problems. It can make you feel more confident about using the phone.

# 4
## Taking control

 a) Ogniana has decided to call Martin. Listen to their phone conversation. What do they talk about?

b) Ogniana has some problems understanding Martin. Listen again. What does she do when she doesn't understand him?

c) Which of the responses below could you use in these situations?

| Situation | Response |
|---|---|
| 1  You didn't understand something the speaker said. | |
| 2  You want to check you understood a piece of information. | |
| 3  You don't know a particular word or phrase the speaker used. | |
| 4  You don't know how to write a word the speaker used. | |

### Responses

a) Sorry, what did you say?

b) I'm sorry, I didn't quite catch that.

c) I'm sorry, could you repeat that, please?

d) OK, let me check I've got that.

e) Could you speak a little more slowly, please?

f) Could you say that again, please?

g) OK, so that's ...

h) Did you say ...?

i) What is ...?

j) I'm sorry, I don't know what ... means.

k) Let me repeat that.

l) Could you spell that please?

m) How do you spell that?

 d) Listen to the cassette and practise saying the responses until you feel satisfied you can use them.

e) Work with a partner and practise taking control. Work in pairs. Your teacher will give each of you a text to read. Don't show it to your partner.

Partner A: Read your text to your partner.
Partner B: Write down the complete text. You can stop the reading to ask your partner to repeat, speak more slowly, spell words etc. When finished, read back the text to your partner to check that it is correct.

How well did you do?

# 5
## It's your choice!

### a) Leaving messages

Leave messages for different class members on an answering machine or tape recorder.

### b) Recording an outgoing message

Record your own outgoing message on an answering machine or tape recorder.

### c) Taking control of a phone call

Work with a partner. Sit back to back and 'phone' your partner to explain how to get to your place for a party. Your partner should note down the instructions. Take it in turns.

### d) Tips for talking on the phone with a native speaker

Write a list of tips for having a successful telephone conversation in English.

### e) Roleplay

Work with a partner. One of you is Martin and the other is a woman who has replied to his ad. Roleplay the telephone conversation when Martin calls to have a chat and to suggest a meeting place.

# 6
## Feedback

How well did you do? What will you do to improve the skills you practised?

| Activity | Comments | To do |
|---|---|---|
| 1  Meeting new people | | |
| 2  Making contact | | |
| 3  Dealing with an answering machine | | |
| 4  Taking control | | |
| 5  It's your choice! | | |

**In Self-study Workbook Unit 19**
Reading comprehension; test yourself – can you take control?; past progressive.

**Grammar**
'Will' for predictions and
spontaneous decisions
to act; 'going to' + verb
for intentions.

**Speaking**
Asking and talking about
the future: predictions,
intentions and
spontaneous decisions
to act.

**Listening**
Listening for detail.

**Learner training**
Practice in self-direction;
setting short-term goals;
self-assessment.

# 1
## Where will you be?

It's the end of this course! With
a partner or in a group, ask and
answer the following questions:

a)  Where will you be this time next week?

b)  Where will you be this time next month?

c)  Where will you be this time next year?

# 2
## Ellie's future

a)  Listen to Karen talking about
her daughter, Ellie. Tick (✓) the
things that Karen predicts.

☐ a) Ellie will travel around the world.

☐ b) The world will be very different in 25 years.

☐ c) There will be more jobs for women.

☐ d) Ellie will be very tough.

☐ e) Ellie won't get a good job.

☐ f) Ellie will be creative, like her father.

☐ g) Ellie will be very rich and successful.

☐ h) Ellie won't go to university.

☐ i) Ellie probably won't get married.

☐ j) Ellie will have many boyfriends.

☐ k) Ellie won't be attractive, like her mother.

☐ l) Ellie will be quite sporty.

☐ m) Ellie won't be short, like her mother.

☐ n) Karen will probably be a grandma.

b)  What do you think life in your
country will be like 25 years from
now? Discuss this in a group.

# 3
## Uses of 'will'

When is 'will' used for the future?
With a partner, look at these
sentences below and decide
whether they are type A or type B.

**Type A**

'Will/won't' is used when you
make a prediction about the future.

**Type B**

'Will/won't' is used when you
make a decision *now* to do
something.

| Sentence | A or B? |
|---|---|
| a  The phone's ringing! I'll answer it. | |
| b  There will be rain in the south east tomorrow. | |
| c  They'll miss you. | |
| d  Put your money away! I'll pay! | |
| e  She won't be late. | |
| f  It's hot in here. I think I'll open the window. | |

## 4
### Good intentions: 'going to' + verb

You've decided to change your lifestyle and become more healthy. What are you going to do? Make a list.

Compare intentions with a partner.

When will you begin your new lifestyle? Maybe next week? Maybe next month? Maybe tomorrow? Sometime in the next six months?

**Activate your grammar**
**'(Be) going to' + verb for future intentions**

We're going to have a holiday soon.
I'm going to start jogging regularly.
We're going to go to New York one day.

➡ See Grammar Review 29 on page 80.

## 5
### Phil's retirement

It's 2021 and Phil is retiring next month after 25 years of working as a graphic designer at the same company.

Listen to Phil talking about his retirement and make a list of his intentions.

## 6
### Your intentions

Research shows that in less than one week you will forget about 80 per cent of everything you have learnt in this unit!

What are you going to do to make sure you don't forget your English?

What are you going to do to improve your English after this course?

# 7
## It's your choice!

Choose the activity you think will be most useful or interesting for you.

### Class survey

Prepare a survey sheet. Choose a topic (e.g. next weekend, your next holiday, when you retire).

Find out what the people in your class plan or intend to do then.

Prepare a report.

### Discussion or writing

What are your predictions for your life or your children's lives in the future? Where will you/they be and what will you/they be doing 10 years or 25 years from now?

Tell the class or read out your predictions.

### Writing: New Year's resolutions

Imagine it is the start of a new year. Make a list of resolutions about all the things you intend or don't intend to do; for example:

I'm going to visit my mother more often.

Show your list to someone else if you want to.

# 8
## Feedback

Did you have any problems with this unit? What are you going to do to help yourself?

| Activity | Problem | Solution |
|---|---|---|
| 1  Where will you be? | | |
| 2  Ellie's future | | |
| 3  Uses of 'will' | | |
| 4  Good intentions | | |
| 5  Phil's retirement | | |
| 6  Your intentions | | |
| 7  It's your choice! | | |

In Self-study
**Workbook Unit 20**
Reading comprehension; intentions: more practice with 'going to'.

# REVIEW 4 Units 16-20

## A

### Progress check

Do these activities to check your progress.

### 1(a) Wordsearch

How many words for describing food can you find? You can read them vertically (↓), diagonally (↘), forwards (→) and backwards (←).

*Check your answers from the Answer Key. Score 3 points for each word you find. (Maximum score is 42 points.)*

| H | A | P | P | E | T | I | S | I | N | G |
|---|---|---|---|---|---|---|---|---|---|---|
| O | O | B | U | T | T | E | R | Y | I | O |
| P | M | T | I | C | K | Y | I | E | C | F |
| C | R | Z | M | B | L | Y | D | N | E | E |
| F | O | S | A | L | T | Y | U | R | B | Y |
| R | R | I | N | O | J | U | I | C | Y | U |
| E | P | E | P | P | E | R | Y | O | K | C |
| T | Y | L | S | M | O | T | A | S | T | Y |
| T | E | F | O | H | S | W | E | E | T | D |
| I | Z | S | U | O | I | C | I | L | E | D |
| B | P | O | R | Y | S | P | I | C | Y | D |

### 1(b) Comparatives and superlatives

Now write down the comparative and superlative forms of each of the adjectives you found in 1(a).

*Check your answers from the Answer Key. Score 4 points for each correct form. Take off 2 points for any spelling mistake.*

### 2 In the restaurant: roleplay

Work with a partner. Choose one of the menus in Unit 17. You are in a restaurant to eat a meal together. Discuss and choose food from the menu, make comments about the meal and finish by asking the waiter for the bill.

*Discuss and agree your score with your partner. Give yourself up to 20 points for fluency and 20 points for correctness and use of language.*

### 3 Gap fill

Fill in the gaps in the text below with appropriate verbs in either the present perfect or the simple past, as appropriate:

I (a) _____ in Melbourne since 1968. My parents are English, however. They (b) _____ in Australia since 1965. I (c) _____ at school in Melbourne from 1973 to 1980. After that I (d) _____ a job as a sales assistant in a furniture shop. I (e) _____ it so much I stayed and I (f) _____ there for over ten years now. I (g) _____ my wife at a barbecue in 1985 and we (h) _____ married for six years. We (i) _____ our wedding anniversary last week. We (j) _____ in this house all our married life. We hope to start a family soon.

*Check your answers from the Answer Key. Score 5 points for each grammatically correct answer. Take off 3 points for each spelling mistake. Add 5 points each for using any of the verbs shown in brackets in the Answer Key.*

Score

1(a) Wordsearch

1(b) Comparatives and superlatives

2 In the restaurant: roleplay

3 Gap fill

## Score

**4 Taking control** ☐

**5 Keep talking** ☐

## 4 Taking control

How many different phrases can you think of to use in the following situations?

a) You haven't understood what someone has said to you.

b) You want someone to repeat what they said to you.

c) You want to check that you have taken down a telephone number correctly.

*Check your answers from the Key. Give yourself 4 points for each suitable and polite phrase, 2 points for each informal phrase. Take off 1 point for each spelling mistake.*

## 5 Keep talking

Work with a partner. Ask and talk about your lives. Start with the past and then talk about the present and the future. Say what you have done, what you are doing and what you will do or intend to do. Talk about work, family, holidays, language learning, retirement etc. How long can you keep talking?

*Give yourselves 5 points each for every minute your conversation lasts. Subtract 1 point for every 20 seconds of hesitation or silence.*

# B
## Checklist

| I can | yes/no |
|---|---|
| describe how food looks, feels, smells and tastes | |
| say how much food I want | |
| understand menus better | |
| order food in a restaurant | |
| say what I don't eat and why | |
| say what has happened recently | |
| talk about my achievements | |
| take control of a conversation | |
| leave messages on an answering machine | |
| talk about my intentions | |
| make predictions about the future | |

| I know | yes/no |
|---|---|
| the difference between mass and count nouns | |
| the form of comparatives and superlatives | |
| the form and some uses of the present perfect | |
| some differences between the present perfect and simple past | |
| two uses of 'will/won't' | |
| which learning activities I like | |
| some of my learning problems | |

# C
## Personal plan

**Problems**

**Plans**

# GRAMMAR REVIEW

## Unit 1
## 1 Questions in the present simple

| Verb 'to be' | Subject | Adjective | Yes/no short answer |
|---|---|---|---|
| Are | you | German?<br>Malaysian?<br>tired? | Yes, I am.<br>No, I'm not. |
| Is | he<br>she | Singaporean?<br>Portuguese? | Yes, he is.<br>No, she isn't.<br>       is not. |

| Auxiliary verb | Subject | Infinitive | | Yes/no short answer |
|---|---|---|---|---|
| Do | you | come<br>like<br>speak<br>write | here often?<br>chocolate?<br>Italian?<br>Chinese? | Yes, I do.<br>No, I don't. |
| Does | she<br>he | like<br>collect | jazz?<br>stamps? | Yes, she does.<br>No, he doesn't. |
| | it | snow | in winter? | Yes, it does.<br>No, it doesn't. |

| 'Wh-'question word | Auxiliary | Subject | Infinitive |
|---|---|---|---|
| Where | do | you<br>they | come from?<br>live?<br>work? |
| | does | he/she<br>Walter | |
| What | do | you<br>they | do?<br>wear to work?<br>think? |
| | does | she/he<br>Laurence | |

**Meaning**
We use questions in the present simple tense mainly for:
1  present states and personal attitudes:
    Are you Chinese?
    Do you like Berlin?
2  habits and repeated actions:
    What does she have for breakfast?
    Does she cook Indian curries often?

**Some common errors**
(**X**) Where you come from?    (✔) Where do you come from?
(**X**) Are you speak Arabic?    (✔) Do you speak Arabic?
    A: Is she French?
(**X**) B: Yes she's.    (✔) Yes, she is.

## Unit 2
## 2 'Can/can't'

| Modal | Subject | Infinitive | Object | Yes/no short answer |
|---|---|---|---|---|
| Can | you<br>he/she<br>Kristina | say | 'hello' in French?<br>'thank you' in Mandarin?<br>'goodbye' in Japanese? | Yes, I can.<br>No, he/she can't. |

| Subject | Auxiliary | Infinitive | Object |
|---|---|---|---|
| I<br>You<br>He/She<br>François | can | order | a meal in Japanese.<br>a taxi in Spanish. |

**Meaning**
'Can' means 'have the ability to'.

**Some common errors**
    A: Can you speak Cantonese?
(**X**) B: Can.    (✔) Yes, I can.
(**X**) Can you to read Greek?    (✔) Can you read Greek?

## 3 'Want to/need to'

| Subject | Verb | Infinitive with 'to' | Object | |
|---|---|---|---|---|
| I | want<br>need | to learn<br>to study | English<br>German<br>Arabic | so that I can travel.<br>in order to get a good job.<br>in order to do business. |
| He/She<br>Thomas<br>The student | needs<br>wants | to learn<br>to study<br>to write | English<br>Russian<br>Japanese | so that he/she can travel.<br>in order to get a good job.<br>in order to do business. |

**Meaning**
'Want to' is used to express a wish or desire:
    I want to marry a millionaire.
'Need to' is used for necessity. If you don't do it there may be a bad consequence:
    I need to visit the dentist.
    She needs to learn French to keep her job.

**Some common errors**
(**X**) I want learn English.    (✔) I want to learn English.
(**X**) Why you want to learn Swedish?    (✔) Why do you want to learn Swedish?

# Unit 3
## 4 Adjectives

| Subject | Verb 'to be' | Adjective |
|---------|--------------|-----------|
| It<br>He<br>She | is/'s | disgusting.<br>boring.<br>amazing. |
| They | are/'re | |

| Subject | Verb 'to be' | Adjective | Prepositional phrase |
|---------|--------------|-----------|----------------------|
| I | am/'m | bored<br>disgusted | by it.<br>with it.<br>with Hong Kong.<br>with television. |
| He<br>She | is/'s | | |
| You/We<br>They | are/'re | tired | of it.<br>of London. |

**Meaning**
We often use adjectives for describing things we like or don't like. Adjectives can tell people what we think.

**Some common errors**

(X) I'm boring with Athens.

(✔) I'm bored with Athens.

(X) I'm interesting in Buddhism.

(✔) I'm interested in Buddhism.

(X) I bored with television.

(✔) I'm bored with television.

# Unit 5
## 5 Comparisons

| Subject | Verb | Comparative adjective | Comparing word | Object |
|---------|------|-----------------------|----------------|--------|
| He/She<br>Sophie<br>Ahmed<br>My sister | is/'s | younger<br>taller<br>more intelligent<br>richer | than | me.<br>him.<br>her.<br>Carla. |
| Australia | | bigger | | New Zealand. |

**Meaning**
We use comparisons when talking about the way things are similar or different.

**Some common errors**

(X) She's more younger than me.

(✔) She's younger than me.

## 6 'Have got/has got'

| Subject | Verb | | Object |
|---------|------|------|--------|
| That woman<br>He/She<br>Annika | has/'s | got | brown hair.<br>black hair.<br>long hair.<br>bad breath.<br>a problem. |
| I<br>You<br>We<br>They | have/'ve | | |

**Meaning**
We use 'have got/has got' to indicate possession. We can also say 'I have/she has'.

**Some common errors**

(X) We got a problem with money.

(✔) We've got a problem with money.

# Unit 6
## 7 Present simple for habitual actions: statements

**Positive**

| Subject | Adverb of frequency | Verb | Adverbial |
|---------|---------------------|------|-----------|
| I<br>You<br>We<br>They | sometimes<br>usually<br>always<br>never | wake up<br>get up<br>arrive | early.<br>late.<br>at 8 o'clock.<br>on time. |
| He/She<br>Joey | | wakes up<br>gets up<br>arrives | |

**Meaning**
We use the present simple to say how often we do something or to describe our routines.

**Some common errors**

(X) I usually to wake up early.

(✔) I usually wake up early.

(X) Azumi often go to bed late.

(✔) Azumi often goes to bed late.

**Negative**

| Subject | Auxiliary | Adverb of frequency | Infinitive | Adverbial |
|---------|-----------|---------------------|------------|-----------|
| I<br>You<br>We<br>They | don't | usually<br>always | wake up<br>get up<br>arrive | early.<br>late.<br>at 8 o'clock.<br>on time. |
| He/She | doesn't | | | |

# 8 Present simple for habitual actions: questions

| 'Wh-' question word | Auxiliary | Subject | (Adverb of frequency) | Infinitive | |
|---|---|---|---|---|---|
| When<br>What time | do | you<br>they | (usually)<br>(generally) | get up?<br>get<br>wake up? | to class? |
| | does | he/she<br>Nicolai | | go | to bed? |
| What | do | you<br>they | (usually)<br>(generally) | do<br>do<br>eat | at the weekend?<br>in the evenings?<br>for breakfast? |
| How | do | you<br>they | (usually)<br>(generally) | get<br>come | to work?<br>to class? |

| | | | Verb | Adverbial |
|---|---|---|---|---|
| Why | do | you | get up<br>go to bed | early every day?<br>so often? |

# Unit 7
# 9 Simple past: regular verbs

| Subject | Verb + '-ed' | Adverb/object | Adverbial |
|---|---|---|---|
| I<br>You<br>He/She<br>They<br>Fatimah | worked<br>arrived | hard<br>early | yesterday.<br>this morning.<br>on Saturday.<br>last month. |
| | started | work | |
| | played | tennis | |
| | learned | French | at school. |

**Meaning**
We use simple past verbs for finished actions that took place in the past.

**Common error**
(X) I work hard yesterday.      (✔) I worked hard yesterday.

# 10 Simple past: irregular verbs

| Subject | Irregular verb | Adverbial | Adverbial (time) |
|---|---|---|---|
| I<br>He/She<br>Martin<br>My girlfriend | was | there<br>in Paris<br>at home<br>on holiday | last week.<br>on Wednesday.<br>yesterday.<br>a month ago. |
| We<br>You<br>They<br>The students | were | | |
| We | went | to the cinema<br>to a rock concert | |
| He | thought | about the problem<br>about his girlfriend | all day.<br>all the time. |

**Common error**
(X) We go to the zoo yesterday.      (✔) We went to the zoo yesterday.

# Unit 8
# 11 Simple past: 'wh-' questions

| 'Wh-' question word | Auxiliary | Subject | Infinitive |
|---|---|---|---|
| What | did | he/she<br>Piak<br>you<br>they | do? |
| Where | | | go?<br>stay? |
| How | | | feel?<br>cope? |

**Some common errors**
(X) Where you go last night?      (✔) Where did you go last night?
(X) Where you went yesterday?      (✔) Where did you go yesterday?

| 'Wh-' question word | Verb 'to be' | Subject | Adjective |
|---|---|---|---|
| Why | were | you<br>we<br>they | late?<br>so late?<br>so early?<br>so tired? |
| | was | he/she<br>Sabina | |

**Common error**
(X) Why you so late yesterday?      (✔) Why were you so late yesterday?

| 'Wh-' question word (subject) | Verb | |
|---|---|---|
| Who | was | Steve?<br>that?<br>there? |
| | were | those people? |
| What | happened? | to you?<br>to your arm? |

## 12 Simple past: yes/no questions

| Auxiliary | Subject | Infinitive | Object | Yes/no short answer |
|---|---|---|---|---|
| Did<br>Didn't | you | see<br>ring | Fred?<br>her/him? | Yes, I did.<br>No, I didn't. |
| | he<br>Thomas | have | a coffee?<br>a glass of wine? | Yes, he did.<br>No, he didn't. |

| Verb 'to be' | Pronoun | Adverbial | Yes/no short answer |
|---|---|---|---|
| Were<br>Weren't | you | at the cinema?<br>at home?<br>in the kitchen?<br>with Tony?<br>there?<br>at home? | Yes, I was.<br>No, I wasn't. |
| | they | | Yes, they were.<br>No, they weren't. |
| Was<br>Wasn't | he/she<br>Ingrid<br>Lek | | Yes, he/she was.<br>No, he/she wasn't. |

**Common error**
(X) Did you went to Rome last year?　(✔) Did you go to Rome last year?

# Unit 9
## 13 Adjectives and adverbs

**Meaning**
Adjectives: See Grammar Review 4.
Adverbs: We use them to modify or give more information about the verb.
Note: We do not generally put adverbs between the verb and the object.

**Some common errors**
(X) He finished quickly his work.　(✔) He finished his work quickly.
(X) She ate the food fastly.　(✔) She ate the food fast.

# Unit 10
## 14 Simple past: modal verbs

| Subject | Past modal | Infinitive | Adverbial | | Present modal |
|---|---|---|---|---|---|
| I | couldn't | swim | last year. | Now I | can. |
| He | had to | go | to Paris last year. | Now he | must go to Brussels. |

**Meaning**
We use modal verbs when events are likely, unlikely, possible, impossible, necessary or not necessary.

**Form**
Modal verbs are irregular verbs and change their form in the simple past.

**Common error**
(X) I can't eat yesterday.　(✔) I couldn't eat yesterday.

# Unit 11
## 15 Question tags

| Positive sentence | Negative question tag |
|---|---|
| It's a nice day,<br>It was a good party,<br>She likes fish,<br>They left early, | isn't it?<br>wasn't it?<br>doesn't she?<br>didn't they? |

| Negative sentence | Positive question tag |
|---|---|
| They aren't English,<br>It hasn't rained for weeks,<br>You don't come here often,<br>The bus won't be late again, | are they?<br>has it?<br>do you?<br>will it? |

**Meaning**
A question tag means 'Is this true or not?'. Sometimes it's a real question, sometimes it's a way of confirming what we already know or of making conversation.

**Some common errors**
(X) She's Korean, isn't it?　(✔) She's Korean, isn't she?
(X) There's a party tonight, is it?　(✔) There's a party tonight, isn't there?

## 16 Present progressive for actions in the present

| Subject | Verb 'to be' | '-ing' verb | |
|---|---|---|---|
| I | am/'m | going | to my English class. |
| He<br>Dirk | is/'s | doing<br>studying | his assignment.<br>Spanish right now. |
| They | are/'re | waiting | for you. |

| Subject | Negative verb 'to be' | '-ing' verb | |
|---|---|---|---|
| The queue | isn't | getting | any shorter! |
| They | aren't | watching | the football on TV. |

| Verb 'to be' | Subject | '-ing' verb | |
|---|---|---|---|
| Is | your husband | working<br>getting | now?<br>ready for the party? |
| Are | the twins | | |

**Meaning**
We use the present progressive for actions that are happening at the moment of speaking.

**Some common errors**
(X) Are you coming from Holland?
(✔) Do you come from Holland?
(X) Are you feel better?
(✔) Are you feeling better?
(X) She going to her Italian class now.
(✔) She's going to her Italian class now.

# Unit 12
## 17 Structures with gerunds and nouns

| | Noun |
|---|---|
| What about<br>How about<br>Do you fancy | a swim?<br>a nice cup of tea? |
| | **Gerund** |
| | coming for a swim?<br>going home? |

**Meaning**
Gerunds (e.g. 'coming', 'going', 'listening') are sometimes called verbal nouns, as they are 'things' like nouns and act like nouns.

**Common error**
(X) What about go to Piccadilly Circus?
(✔) What about going to Piccadilly Circus?

## 18 Past progressive for invitations

| Subject | Verb 'to be' (past) | '-ing' verb | |
|---|---|---|---|
| I<br>Kim | was | wondering | whether you'd like a coffee.<br>if you wanted to come tonight.<br>whether you'd like to go as well. |
| We | were | thinking | you might like to eat Greek food tonight. |

**Meaning**
We use the past progressive for thinking/wondering, even though the action of thinking is taking place now.

**Common error**
(X) I am thinking you might like a curry.
(✔) I was thinking you might like a curry.

## 19 Present progressive for future plans

| Subject | Verb 'to be' | '-ing' verb | |
|---|---|---|---|
| I | am/'m | going<br>flying | to Amsterdam this weekend.<br>to Paris on Monday.<br>to Bangkok tomorrow night. |
| She<br>Katrin | is/'s | | |
| We<br>They | are/'re | babysitting<br>cooking | tomorrow. |

**Meaning**
The present progressive is used to talk about fixed plans in the future.

**Common error**
(X) We are go to Paris tomorrow.
(✔) We are going to Paris tomorrow.

# Unit 13
## 20 Imperatives

| (Subject) | Imperative | Adverbial/object |
|---|---|---|
| (You) | Turn | left/right. |
| | Keep | to the left-/right-hand side.<br>going. |
| | Don't go | in there! |

**Meaning**
We use imperatives to tell people very directly to do certain things.

**Common error**
(X) You turning to the left here.
(✔) You turn to the left here.
(X) You no take the bus.
(✔) Don't take the bus.

# Unit 14
## 21 'Must', 'have to', 'don't have to'

**Positive**

| Subject | | Infinitive | Object | |
|---|---|---|---|---|
| You | must | try<br>have | one of these cakes!<br>some retsina.<br>this taco sauce. | } Telling people what to do. |
| I<br>We | have to<br>must | be | going soon.<br>leaving now. | } Obligation. |
| He/She | has to<br>must | leave | early. | |

**Negative**

| You | don't have to | eat<br>drink<br>be<br>leave | it if you don't want to.<br>the retsina if you don't like it.<br>going yet.<br>early. |
|---|---|---|---|
| She | doesn't have to | | |
| We | mustn't | be | late. |

**Meaning**

We use 'must / have to' for actions that are necessary. The meanings are similar, but we usually use 'must' when we tell people what to do. We often use 'have to' when we talk about obligation.

**Common error**

(X) I don't must finish it before next week.　　(✔) I don't have to finish it before next week.

# Unit 16
## 22 Count and mass nouns

**Meanings**

Count nouns are items like eggs that you can count ('one egg', 'two eggs' etc.). Mass nouns are items like milk that you cannot count. Note that you can count coins ('I've got three 20p coins') and notes ('She's got ten £20 notes') but that 'money' is considered a mass noun, uncountable.

**Some common errors**

(X) Do you want a bread?　　(✔) Do you want some bread?

(X) Have you got many money?　　(✔) Have you got much money?

## 23 'Too' and 'not enough'

| Subject | Verb | | Adjective | |
|---|---|---|---|---|
| Chocolate<br>Thai food<br>Greek food | is | too | sweet<br>hot<br>oily | for me.<br>for him.<br>for Hakan. |

| Subject | Negative | Adjective | | |
|---|---|---|---|---|
| Chinese food<br>Strawberries without sugar | isn't<br>aren't | spicy<br>sweet | enough | for me.<br>for Mr Patel. |

**Some common errors**

(X) Turkish delight is very too sweet for me.　　(✔) Turkish delight is too sweet for me.

(X) She has too much money to live in Tokyo.　　(✔) She has enough money to live in Tokyo.

## 24 Comparatives: '-er', 'less than', 'more than', 'as ... as'

| | Subject | Verb | | Adjective | | |
|---|---|---|---|---|---|---|
| This | cheese pizza | is | less<br>more | creamy<br>delicious<br>expensive | than | that one. |
| These | cakes | are | | | | those ones. |

| | Subject | Negative | | Adjective | | |
|---|---|---|---|---|---|---|
| This | avocado | isn't | as | tasty<br>cheap | as | that one. |
| These | grapes<br>watermelons<br>mangoes | aren't | | | | those ones. |

**Meaning**

We use comparatives to compare one thing with another.

**Form**

Adjectives with one syllable: add '-er'. Adjectives ending in '-y': add '-ier'. Adjectives with three or more syllables: add 'more' + adjective.

**Common error**

(X) This red wine isn't tasty as that one.　　(✔) This red wine isn't as tasty as that one.

# Unit 17
## 25 'Some/any'; 'something/anything'

| Subject | (Negative) | Infinitive | | Object |
|---|---|---|---|---|
| I | (don't) | like<br>eat | some<br>any<br>anything | seafood.<br>food with garlic in it.<br>with meat in it. |

| Have | you<br>we/they | got | any<br>some | Chinese tea?<br>oysters? |
|---|---|---|---|---|

| Subject +<br>'would' | Infinitive | | Adjective | |
|---|---|---|---|---|
| I'd | like | something | sweet<br>spicy<br>chocolaty | for dessert.<br>for the main course.<br>after the main course. |

**Meaning**
'Some' and 'any' describe quantities and they can both be used with mass or count nouns. 'Any' (and 'anything') is most often used with negatives and questions:
    We haven't got any milk (= we have none at all.)
However, 'some' (and 'sometimes') can also be used with negatives and questions when we want to suggest that the quantity is <u>limited</u> in some way:
    I don't like some modern buildings (= certain ones. I do like others.)
    Have you got some paper I can use? (= a certain limited amount.)

## 26 Superlatives

| | Definite article | Superlative | Noun | |
|---|---|---|---|---|
| It was | the | hottest<br>spiciest<br>most expensive<br>most delicious<br>worst | meal<br>food<br>pizza<br>soup | I've ever had. |

**Meaning**
We use superlatives to say something has more of a particular quality than all other things.

**Form**
Adjectives with one syllable: add '-est'. Adjectives ending in '-y': add '-iest'. Adjectives with three or more syllables: add 'most' + adjective.

**Common error**
(X) It was the most hottest food I've ever tasted.　(✔) It was the hottest food I've ever tasted.

# Unit 18
## 27 Present perfect: questions

| | | (Adverb) | Past participle | |
|---|---|---|---|---|
| Have | you | (ever)<br>(already) | eaten<br>met<br>been<br>missed<br>sung<br>been | lobster?<br>my partner?<br>to America?<br>an appointment?<br>in a Karaoke lounge?<br>to a Puccini opera? |
| Has | he/she<br>Roberta<br>Faisal | | | |

**Meaning**
We use present perfect questions to enquire about an action completed at any time in the past. The word 'ever' is used to mean 'in all your life'.

**Some common errors**
(X) Have you seen your sister last week?　(✔) Did you see your sister last week?
A: Have you ever been to Vietnam?
(X) B: Yes, I ever.　(✔) Yes, I have.

# Unit 19
## 28 Past progressive

| Subject | Verb 'to be' (past) | '-ing' verb | | Simple past |
|---|---|---|---|---|
| I | was | looking<br>thinking | through the replies<br>about you | and I liked your letter.<br>and I decided to write. |
| We<br>They | were | eating<br>watching | dinner<br>a video | when the phone rang.<br>when there was a knock at the door. |

**Meaning**
We use the past progressive for longer actions in the past. The word 'when' indicates an interruption, which is usually described in the simple past.

**Common error**
(X) We were watching the football on TV when the phone was ringing.　(✔) We were watching the football on TV when the phone rang.

# Unit 20
## 29 '(Be) going to' + verb for future intentions

| Subject | Verb 'to be' | | Infinitive | Object |
|---|---|---|---|---|
| We<br>They | are/'re | going to | have<br>go<br>start<br><br>buy | a holiday soon.<br>to New York one day.<br>jogging soon.<br>learning the guitar next year.<br>some CDs this afternoon. |
| I | am/'m | | | |
| He/she<br>Petra | is | | | |

**Meaning**
We use 'going to' for intentions in the future.

**Some common errors**
(X) She's going to shopping later.　(✔) She's going to go shopping later.
(X) We going to dance all night.　(✔) We're going to dance all night.

# ANSWER KEY

## Unit 3 Exercise 2

| | |
|---|---|
| + + + + + | I really love it. |
| + + + + | I love it. |
| + + + | I like it very much. |
| + + | I like it. |
| + | I quite like it. |
| n | I'm not sure. |
| − | I don't like it very much. |
| − − | I don't like it. |
| − − − | I don't like it at all. |
| − − − − | I hate it. |
| − − − − − | I really hate it. |

## Unit 4 Exercise 1(b)

Denpasar is north-east of Kuta.
Kuta is south-west of Denpasar.

Fortaleza is in the north of Brazil.
It is north-west of Recife.

Recife is in the east of Brazil.
It is south-east of Fortaleza.

Kyoto is north-east of Kobe.
Kobe is south-west of Kyoto.

## Unit 5 Exercise 2(c)

**Information**
divorced   single   mid-thirties   widow   Londoner

**Appearance**
brunette   slim   well-built   sporty   blonde   beard
red-haired   handsome

**Qualities**
cheerful   hard-working   bad-tempered   nosey
intelligent   friendly

**Interests**
cinema   football

## Unit 6 Exercise 3

Suggested answers:

a) When/What time does Joey (always) wake up?
b) What does Louise do at 7.30 am?
c) When do Louise and Joey get home?
d) When does Louise spend more time with Joey?
e) What does Louise (usually) eat for lunch?
f) What does Louise (usually) eat in the evening?
g) When is Louise's lunch break?
   When does Louise have lunch?
   When does Louise do her shopping?
h) When does Louise catch the train home?
i) How long do Joey and Louise play together in the
   evening?
   How long does Louise play with Joey in the evening?
j) When does Louise go to bed?

## Unit 6 Exercise 4

a) Five thirty am; five thirty pm; half past five in the
   morning; half past five in the afternoon; seventeen
   thirty.
b) Twelve noon; noon; twelve midnight; midnight;
   twenty-four hundred hours.

c) Six forty-five am; six forty-five pm; a quarter to
   seven in the morning; a quarter to seven in the
   evening; eighteen forty-five.
d) One oh one am; one oh one pm; one minute past one
   in the morning; one minute past one at night; one
   minute past one in the afternoon; thirteen oh one.

## Unit 6 Exercise 6

always   usually   often   sometimes   rarely   never

## Unit 7 Exercise 4

I **was** born in 1947 in Shanghai. In 1950 my parents
**brought** me and my three brothers to Taiwan to live. We
**lived** in Kaohsiung, near the sea. My mother and father,
now dead, **made** prawn mee (noodles) and **sold** it to
workers in the town. It **was a** hard life. I **didn't** go to
school until I **was** 10. I **studied** very hard and **got** a job
in a shop when I **was** 16. **In** March 1966 I **got** married
to Harry. We **got a** flat in town. Harry is **a** sailor. His
parents **came** from Beijing in 1932. **On** 9 April 1970 we
**had a/our** son, Kelvin. Last year we **travelled** to Australia
and New Zealand. We **liked** it very much.

## Unit 8 Exercise 1(a)

Suggested answers:

1 They are boyfriend and girlfriend.
2 They don't live near each other; they can't see each
  other very often; Joe is jealous.

## Unit 8 Exercise 1(b)

Suggested answers:

1 She worked overtime.
2 Mr Williams asked her to because of the sales
  conference.
3 He was her boss, Mr Williams, the new director.
4 He asked her out to dinner after work.
5 They ate at an Italian restaurant and then he drove her
  home as it was late. She asked him in for a coffee. He
  drank his coffee and then went home.
6 He felt angry and jealous.
7 She felt angry because Joe didn't trust her.

## Unit 8 Exercise 5

See Tapescript Unit 8, Learning tip (b).

## Unit 9 Exercise 2

a) Annette, China (Guilin)
b) Bill, Indonesia (Java)
c) Not mentioned
d) Marti, Malaysia (Rawa)

## Unit 9 Exercise 3

The Great Barrier Reef, Australia.

## Unit 10 Exercise 2

1 (b)   2 (c)   3 (a)

## Review 2 Exercise 1

a) False. She **sometimes** starts work at 7 am.
b) False. Helen generally comes in **before** 9 am.
c) True.
d) True.
e) True.
f) True.
g) False. Most of the post is **usually** for Helen.
h) False. She **always** checks the newspapers.
i) True.
j) False. She **rarely** goes on business trips abroad
   with Helen.
k) True.
l) False: She generally leaves **between 6.00 and 6.30.**

## Unit 11 Exercise 2

Suggested answers:

**1   Carmen and a woman in a supermarket queue**
    Carmen probably doesn't know the woman at all
    or only a little.

**2   Carmen and her English friend's parent**
    Carmen has never met John's father before.

**3   Carmen and her neighbour**
    Carmen has spoken to her neighbour before.

**4   Carmen and a woman with a baby**
    Carmen has never spoken to this woman before.

## Unit 11 Exercise 4

Suggested answers:

**1   Oh no. This queue is very slow, isn't it?**
    (a) Something neutral: the supermarket queue.

**2   Hello, I'm Carmen. You 're John's father, aren't you?
    John's expecting me.**
    (b) Something connected with the person, but not
    too personal (i.e. John).

**3   Hello, Mrs Wallace. How are you?**
    (b) Something connected with the person, but not
    too personal.

**4   What a lovely baby! She's beautiful!**
    (c) Something very personal (i.e. the woman's
    baby). Notice that the comment is very positive:
    a compliment.

## Unit 11 Exercise 5

See Tapescript Unit 11 Exercise 5.

## Unit 12 Exercise 2

a) Graham and Diana Millington.
b) A housewarming, i.e. to celebrate moving to a
   new house.
c) Formal attire, i.e. a suit and definitely a tie.
d) A partner. (Note: This more neutral term is often
   used now instead of the more specific 'wife',
   'husband', 'live-in lover', 'boyfriend' or 'girlfriend'.
   Since it is a formal occasion, he is not expected to
   bring a bottle (of wine or other alcoholic drink), as is
   usually the case for less formal parties in, say, Britain

or Australia; but it would be polite for him to take a small gift (something for the house would be appropriate) and perhaps some flowers for the hosts.
e) 'Répondez s'il vous plaît', which is French for 'Please reply'. He should let his hosts know in good time whether he is coming and whether he is bringing someone with him.

## Unit 12 Exercise 3(a)

See Tapescript Unit 12, Exercise 3(a).

## Unit 12 Exercise 3(c)

Suggested answers:

| | | | |
|---|---|---|---|
| A 1 | C 2 | E 1 | G 2 |
| B 2 | D 2 | F 1 | |

## Unit 12 Exercise 4

**Pat:** Saturday? Well, I'd love to, but I'm afraid I can't. I'm going to Paris for the weekend.
Pat sounds sincere about wanting to go but not being able to. She emphasises 'I'd love to'.

**Mike:** Oh yeah, great! Let's do that. Mmmm, yes. That'd be super.
Mike is obviously relieved and pleased that Pat wants to see him and readily accepts.

## Unit 13 Exercise 1(a)

The designer has labelled The Rocks Police Station as Doyle's Restaurant, and vice versa.

## Unit 13 Exercise 1(b)

She didn't turn right through the archway to Nurses Walk. Instead, she carried on, past the Fortune of War pub and turned right then.

## Unit 13 Exercise 2

a) 'Hello' is generally used only as a greeting in English-speaking countries. Not appropriate.
b) This might be used in a situation where the person you are trying to stop has annoyed you in some way – perhaps damaged your car, broken a window etc. Not polite.
c) This is a possibility, but **only** sounds polite if the intonation is right. It would probably give the impression of great frustration. Possibly acceptable.
d) Fairly polite, but would sound better with 'Excuse me', as in (e) and (f).
e) Polite.
f) A very polite/formal way of getting someone's attention.
g) Again, very polite/formal.

## Unit 14 Exercise 2

| | | |
|---|---|---|
| a) False | e) True | i) True |
| b) True | f) True | j) False |
| c) True | g) False | k) False |
| d) False | h) True | |

## Unit 14 Exercise 3

'**Would you like …?**' is perhaps most generally useful and could be used with all three.

'**How about …?**' and '**Drink?**' are informal and would be used with someone you know well, like your best friend and, possibly, your daughter's boyfriend.

'**You must have something to drink**' is fairly neutral and could be used with all three.

'**May**' is formal and would be most appropriate with your boss.

The expressions concerning taking a coat are presented from most formal to least formal. '**Give me …**' is generally informal and would be appropriate use with your best friend.

## Unit 14 Exercise 4

Suggested answers:

1  May I use your bathroom?
2  Do you mind if I use your toilet?
3  Could I use your toilet?
4  Can I use your toilet?
5  Where's the loo?

## Unit 15 Exercise 3

1  (c) **'Hello, this is … here.'**
    This is the usual way of stating who you are on the phone in English.

    '**Hello, I'm …**' would be acceptable, if you are introducing yourself for the first time.

2  (c) **'Is that John?'**
    This is the usual way of checking someone's identity on the phone. It corresponds to 'This is …'.

    '**John?**' would also be acceptable, though perhaps less formal.

3  (c) **'Could I speak to John, please?'**
    (d) **'I'd like to speak to John, please.'**
    (e) **'Is John there, please?'**
    All of the above are acceptable. (c) and (d) are most often used in formal situations, such as when making business calls. (e) tends to be used in less formal situations and when the caller expects the person to be there.

4  (c) **'Hold on, please.'**
    (d) **'Just a moment.'** (from 'Please wait just a moment'.)
    Both (c) and (d) are acceptable.

5  (a) **'I'll call back later.'**
    This is grammatically correct. 'I'll' is used because it is a promise of future action.
    (b) is common amongst non-native speakers of English, but incorrect.

6  (c) **'Could I leave a message, please?'**
    (d) **'Could you give him a message, please?'**
    These are both acceptable ways of indicating that you wish to leave a message.

## Unit 15 Exercise 4

a)  Nina appears to be quite close to Ari. A girlfriend?
b)  Jean is upset and probably jealous.
c)  'Sorry Jean, I didn't quite catch that!'
    'Sorry? What did you say?'
d)  Pardon?
    Could you repeat that, please?
    I'm sorry, I didn't hear you/that.
    Sorry, what did you say?
    What? Eh? (informal)

## Unit 15 Exercise 5

Ari is making a booking for a double room in a hotel. He is staying for two nights in May. He is probably taking one of his girlfriends with him.

## Review 3 Exercise 1

The people talking are Carmen and a stranger.

## Review 3 Exercise 5

Suggested answers:

Cross Grand Junction Road and turn left into Old Steine. Go past the bus station and follow Old Steine to the right. Turn left into North Street. Go straight ahead, past the Royal Pavilion on the right, and then take the second

turning on the right, New Road. The Theatre Royal is in New Road, on the left-hand side.

Turn left into Grand Junction Road and take the first street on the right, East Street. Cross Prince Albert Street and keep going up East Street until it joins North Street, near the Royal Pavilion. Turn left into North Street and then take the second turning on the right, New Road. The Theatre Royal is in New Road, on the left-hand side.

## Review 3 Exercise 6

Suggested answers:

a)  Excuse me … Sorry to bother you, but I wonder if I could possibly use your telephone for a moment to make a very urgent call? It won't take long.
b)  Would you mind if I used your bathroom?
    I wonder if I could use your bathroom?
    Could I possibly powder my nose/freshen up/wash my hands?

## Unit 16 Exercise 2(b)

cheese; ham; bread; stuffed olives; duck paté; bacon, lettuce and tomato rolls; tuna rolls; apple juice; grapes.

## Unit 16 Exercise 3(a)

**Count nouns**
Can be counted (e.g. 'one egg', 'two eggs' etc.).

Can take an indefinite article ('a/an').
Can also use 'some/any' with a plural noun.

Can take a singular or plural verb, (e.g. 'These rolls are tasty/This roll is tasty'). With count nouns you ask 'How **many**?' The answer should contain a number (e.g. '**Six** tomatoes, please').

**Mass nouns**
Cannot be counted, e.g you can't say 'three milks' (unless one milk is understood to be a defined amount, such as a glassful in a cafe).

Cannot take an indefinite article – you need to use 'some/any'.

Can only take a singular verb (e.g. 'This cheese is nice').

With mass nouns you ask 'How **much**?' The answer should contain a measurement or a number + a fixed measuring unit (e.g. 'a litre/two bottles/two cartons').

In order to make a mass noun countable, you need to add a fixed measuring unit, (e.g. 'a loaf of bread', 'a piece of cake').

## Unit 16 Exercise 3(b)

**Count nouns**

| | |
|---|---|
| quiche | pancake |
| rolls | chocolate* |
| grapes | lettuce* |
| stuffed olives | sausage* |
| avocado | cheese* |
| tomato | cake* |

**Note**
'Cake(s)' and 'chocolate(s)' are count nouns if the whole item is referred to (e.g. 'a chocolate', 'two cakes').

'Cheese(s)' is a count noun when referring to more than one sort (e.g. 'There are many different cheeses from France'). 'Fish' is the same.

'Lettuce' may be a count noun if the whole vegetable is referred to.

**Mass nouns**

| | |
|---|---|
| bread | duck paté |
| cake | ham |
| orange juice | chocolate* |
| apple juice | lettuce* |
| tuna | sausage* |
| bacon | cheese* |
| mineral water | cake* |

**Note**

'Cake' and 'chocolate' are mass nouns when the quantity is not defined (e.g. 'some cake', 'a piece of chocolate').
'Cheese' is a mass noun when referring to an indefinite sort or amount (e.g. 'I'd like some cheese'). 'Fish' is the same.
'Lettuce' may be a mass noun if no definite quantity is referred to.

## Unit 16 Exercise 4

Suggested answers:

**slice** (thin piece): quiche, cake, paté, tomato, cheese, bacon, sausage, bread, ham, pizza, pie
**piece** (undefined size): cake, pie, quiche, chicken, bread
**bit** (small portion): most food items

## Unit 16 Exercise 5

a) The goat's cheese smelled too strong.
b) The camembert wasn't soft enough.
c) They bought the brie. It tasted great/creamy. A nice, big piece.
d) The avocados weren't soft enough/were too hard.
e) White grapes. They tasted sweeter than the red ones. Two big bunches.

## Unit 16 Exercise 6

a) delicious, disgusting, soft, hard, juicy, creamy, nice
b) disgusting, soft, hard, juicy, nice
c) delicious, disgusting, spicy, buttery, nice
d) delicious, disgusting, juicy, creamy, spicy, hot, buttery, nice

## Unit 17 Exercise 3(a)

Newbery's

## Unit 17 Exercise 3(b)

**Sandra:** mineral water, pancake with caviare, lobster thermidor, salad and rice

**Pete:** apple juice, artichokes, pork with lemon, French beans, new English potatoes

## Unit 17 Exercise 6

'Some' is used when the quantity is limited in some way. For example, 'I don't eat some meat' means that there is a limited amount of meat I don't eat. I do eat certain types of meat.

'Any' is used when the quantity is not limited at all. 'I don't eat any meat' means that I eat none at all: the amount of meat I don't eat is not limited.

'Have you got any oysters?' means 'Have you got any at all?'
'Have you got some oysters?' means 'Have you got a certain number?' (I realise the supply is not unlimited!)

In other words, it is not incorrect to use both 'some' and 'any' in positive and negative statements, as well as questions. However, the meanings will be slightly different.

## Unit 18 Exercise 2

1 (j)   2 (e)   3 (i)

## Unit 18 Exercise 4

The following are incorrect or not usually used:

### a) **I have seen this film last week.**

**Explanation:** Because a specific time in the past is referred to ('last week'), this sentence should be in the simple past: 'I **saw** this film last week.' The action is finished.

In the sentence 'I have seen this film', the focus is on the action of seeing the film and when it was seen is not important.

### c) **He's cleaned the car this morning.**

**Explanation:** See explanation above for (a): 'this morning' is a specific time in the past.

### e) **I was just sick.**

**Explanation:** If the speaker is describing something which has just happened (for example, in response to 'You look terrible! What's the matter?'), then the present perfect should be used: '**I've** just **been** sick.' (Note: In American English the construction with the simple past is more common.)

## Unit 19 Exercise 4(b)

She asks him to speak more slowly.

She explains that her English isn't good.

She asks him to repeat things ('I'm sorry, what did you say?' 'I'm sorry, I didn't quite catch that').

She paraphrases (e.g. 'Sofia' for 'your home town') to check she has understood correctly.

She repeats part of Martin's sentences with the intonation of a question, leaving him to finish them and so repeat words she did not catch ('A good . . .?' 'You loved the . . .?').

She asks for clarification. ('What is estate agent?').

She asks for the spelling of important names.

She repeats information back to Martin to check she has understood it.

## Unit 19 Exercise 4(c)

1 (a), (b), (c), (e), (f)
2 (d), (g), (h), (k)
3 (i), (j)
4 (l), (m)

## Unit 20 Exercise 2(a)

(b), (d), (f), (g), (j), (l), (m), (n)

## Unit 20 Exercise 3

Type A: (b), (c), (e)
Type B: (a), (d), (f)

## Unit 20 Exercise 5

He's going to move to a bungalow in Essex.
He's going to join the British Legion.
He's going to get to know people there.
He's going to start painting again.
He's going to try oil painting.
He's going to read a lot/all the books he never had time to read before.
He's going to go on holiday with his daughter and her husband to Greece.
They're going to fly to Athens and then take a cruise.

## Review 4 Exercise 1(a)

| | | |
|---|---|---|
| appetising | hot | sour |
| bitter | juicy | spicy |
| buttery | nice | sweet |
| dry | peppery | tasty |
| fresh | salty | |

## Review 4 Exercise 1(b)

| Comparatives | Superlatives |
|---|---|
| more appetising | most appetising |
| more bitter/bitterer | most bitter/bitterest |
| more buttery | most buttery |
| drier | driest |
| fresher | freshest |
| hotter | hottest |
| juicier | juiciest |
| nicer | nicest |
| more peppery | most peppery |
| saltier | saltiest |
| sourer | sourest |
| spicier | spiciest |
| sweeter | sweetest |
| tastier | tastiest |

## Review 4 Exercise 3

a) have lived/(have resided)/have been
b) have been/have lived
c) was
d) got/found/started/began/took up/had
e) liked (enjoyed, adored)
f) have been/have worked
g) met (got to know/became acquainted with)
h) have been
i) had/celebrated
j) have been/ have lived (have resided)

## Review 4 Exercise 4

a) I'm sorry, I didn't (quite) catch that.
   I'm sorry, my English isn't very good.
   I'm sorry, that was a little fast for me.
   I'm sorry, what does . . . mean?
   I'm sorry, I don't understand.

   Informal:
   Pardon?
   What was that?
   What?
   Sorry?

b) Could you say that again, please?
   Could you repeat that, please?
   I'm sorry, what was that?

   Informal:
   Say again?
   What was that?
   Say that again.

c) Let me just check I've got it right.
   Let me repeat that.
   So that's . . .
   The number is . . .
   Did you say . . .?
   Was that . . .?

# TAPESCRIPTS

## Unit 1 Exercise 3

**Susan:** Hello. I'm Susan Chan.
**Wolfgang:** Nice to meet you. I'm Wolfgang Simler.
**Susan:** Are you German?
**Wolfgang:** Yes, I am. I'm from Berlin. Where do you come from?
**Susan:** I'm from Malaysia.
**Wolfgang:** Really? How interesting! Are you a flight attendant? Malaysian Airlines, maybe?
**Susan:** No, I'm not. I'm a bank manager.
**Wolfgang:** Oh! Sorry! How interesting!
**Susan:** Yes. What do you do, Wolfgang?
**Wolfgang:** I'm a nurse. I work in a health clinic.
**Susan:** Really! Is it hard work?
**Wolfgang:** Of course. Very hard. Er ... um, do you come here often?
**Susan:** No, this is my first time.
**Wolfgang:** Really? Do you ...

## Unit 2 Exercise 3

**Interviewer:** Why do you want to learn English, Manee?
**Manee:** Well, I want to be a tourist guide in Thailand.
**Interviewer:** Really? That's interesting! What do you need to do?
**Manee:** Well, I need to do everything: understand the tourists' questions, tell them about the things they see, read guidebooks and write information posters for the hotels. I need to learn more words to talk about things, like temples. I want to be a good guide!

## Unit 3 Exercise 3

**Interviewer:** So, Linda, what you think about living in Singapore?
**Linda:** Well, it's OK. I love the weather – it's always hot.
**Greg:** Yeah, I quite like the weather, but sometimes it's too hot and humid.
**Interviewer:** It's a very modern city. Do you like that?
**Greg:** Yes, I like the modern buildings very much. Don't you, Linda?
**Linda:** No, I don't. I hate the skyscrapers! I like the greenery, though. You know, the tropical trees and plants.
**Greg:** Yes, me too.
**Interviewer:** Singapore's a shoppers' paradise, isn't it?
**Linda:** I disagree. I really hate shopping here.
**Greg:** Yeah, I really hate it, too. Too many people.
**Interviewer:** Are there any nice beaches in Singapore?
**Greg:** There are some beaches, but I don't like them much. The water isn't clean.
**Linda:** Oh, I quite like the beach at Changi.
**Greg:** Really? Why?
**Linda:** It has nice sand.
**Interviewer:** What about the night life in Singapore?
**Linda:** Oh, I love the night life. It's great! You can eat, dance, go to the cinema ...
**Greg:** I'm not sure about the night life. There isn't much to do, really, except eat.
**Interviewer:** Do you like the food here?
**Linda:** Oh, I really love it!
**Greg:** So do I. You can have Chinese, Indian, Malay food – everything.
**Interviewer:** What do you think about the people in Singapore?
**Linda:** I like them. They're very friendly.
**Greg:** Yes, I think so, too.

## Unit 4 Exercise 1

1 **Interviewer:** Where do you come from?
**Woman:** Oh, I live in Cairns.
**Interviewer:** Where?
**Woman:** Cairns.
**Interviewer:** Where's that?
**Woman:** It's on the coast of northern Queensland in Australia, near the Great Barrier Reef, right?
**Interviewer:** Oh, sounds wonderful!
**Woman:** Yeah. You can get a boat to the coral reef and go snorkelling.
**Interviewer:** Lovely.

2 **Interviewer:** What about you?
**Man:** Oh, well, we come from Bath.
**Interviewer:** Where's that?
**Man:** It's a city in the south-west of England, about an hour and a half from London by train.
**Interviewer:** Near Bristol?
**Man:** Yes, that's right.
**Interviewer:** Isn't Bath called Bath because it has Roman baths there?
**Man:** Yes, the Romans came to Bath nearly two thousand years ago.
**Interviewer:** Really?

3 **Interviewer:** So, where do you come from, then?
**Man:** Well, my home's in Yakima.
**Interviewer:** Yaki ...?
**Man:** ... ma.Yakima. Do you know where that is?
**Interviewer:** No, I don't. I've never heard of it. Where is it?
**Man:** It's in Washington State in the US. It's a small agricultural town about two hours north-east of Portland, Oregon.
**Interviewer:** What's Yakima famous for?
**Man:** Fruit. Yeah, we grow apples. Nice, big juicy apples.
**Interviewer:** Apples, eh?

## Unit 7 Exercise 3

**Interviewer:** Tell us some more about life on the reservation. Did you live in tents?
**Bernard:** Tents? You mean tepees. No, we didn't. We lived in wooden houses, sometimes with one room, sometimes more. We moved around a lot.
**Interviewer:** What did you eat?
**Bernard:** Well, the government gave us some food, like flour and sugar, and we hunted rabbits and other small animals to eat.
**Interviewer:** Did you live near a town?
**Bernard:** Not really. We lived near Wakpala, a small village with one shop, one street, one church. That's where I went to school.
**Interviewer:** Did you learn Lakhota at school?
**Bernard:** Ha! No, no. I learned Lakhota from my relatives and the other Indians on the reservation. At that time the older Indians only spoke Lakhota. School was in English. If you couldn't understand English you sat at the back of the class. There were no English lessons for kids who couldn't speak it. Sometimes they stayed in one class until they were real big. Most dropped out.
**Interviewer:** But you graduated from high school? Wasn't that very unusual at that time?
**Bernard:** Yeah. I was lucky. My dad spoke English at home, so I was bilingual.
**Interviewer:** Say something in Lakhota for us.
**Bernard:** *Wahiyu cherk'api.* That's my name. It means 'Jerked-with-arrow'.

**Interviewer:** Jerked with arrow? Jerk – you mean to move suddenly?
**Bernard:** Yeah. I was named after a chief who was shot by an arrow and it took a long time to pull the arrow out. I guess his body jerked a lot when they tried to pull it out!
**Interviewer:** Yes. Hmm. Er ... You studied veterinary medicine, didn't you? Was that because you learned a lot about animals when you were young?
**Bernard:** Yes, I guess so. You see, we lived very close to nature. An old Indian called Mad Bear taught me all about horses, how they think and how to tame them.
**Interviewer:** Did Mad Bear speak English?
**Bernard:** No, no, only Lakhota. Anyway, I wanted to use my knowledge and I know I'm good with animals, so I became a veterinarian. We always have animals at home, too. We've got two cats right now.

## Unit 8 Exercise 1

**Lisa:** Hello?
**Joe:** Hi, it's me.
**Lisa:** Joe! Hello, darling. Thanks for calling.
**Joe:** Mmm. How was your week?
**Lisa:** How was my week? Well, it was quite stressful. Mr Williams, you know, the new director, asked me to do overtime every day this week because of the sales conference next week.
**Joe:** Overtime every day? Did he pay you for it?
**Lisa:** Oh yes. He also took me out to dinner on Friday evening.
**Joe:** He took you out to dinner? Where did you go?
**Lisa:** Eh? Oh, that little Italian Restaurant in Duke Street. You know ...
**Joe:** Oh yeah, I know, the dark, romantic one! Did he take you home?
**Lisa:** Take me home? Who? Oh, you mean Steve?
**Joe:** Who's Steve?
**Lisa:** Mr Williams. Yes, he did. Of course, he drove me home. It was late.
**Joe:** Late! Did you ask him in for coffee, then?
**Lisa:** Hang on a minute ...
**Joe:** Did you ask him in?
**Lisa:** Yes, I did. So what?
**Joe:** So, first he took you to dinner, then he drove you home, then he came in for a coffee. What happened next, then?
**Lisa:** Oh for goodness sake! Nothing happened. He drank his coffee and went home. OK?
**Joe:** He went home. OK, sorry. I miss you ...
**Lisa:** I miss you, too. Can you come down next weekend?
**Joe:** Well ...

## Unit 8 Learning tip (a)

And now for today's weather. Expect a mainly sunny day with some scattered showers in the west. There'll be some heavy rain this evening in the west and this will move into the east during the night. Tomorrow's weather will be cool and wet in all areas.

## Unit 8 Learning tip (b)

1 I went to the **shops** and then **I had** some **lunch** and then I **came home.**
2 We **saw** a **film** called *Dances* with *Wolves.*
3 We had a **wonderful** time. We **ate**, **swam** and **lay** in the **sun.**
4 He **entered** the **house** through the **bathroom window** and **took five thousand pounds** from the **safe.**

## Unit 9 Exercise 2

**1 Interviewer:** So, Bill, tell us about your holiday!
**Bill:** Well, I love mountains and volcanoes so I was interested to see the volcanic craters near Lembang in Java.
**Interviewer:** In Java? That's Indonesia, isn't it?
**Bill:** Indonesia, yes, that's right. The weather was quite cool up there, which was good, because we had a long climb to get to the crater. It was still actively throwing out sulphurous fumes. It really stank – just like rotten eggs, you know?
**Interviewer:** Ugh! Yeah.
**Bill:** Well! We had a friendly Indonesian guide and he showed us the naturally boiling water and the hot steam coming out of the ground and he explained everything really well in English.
**Interviewer:** Boiling water and steam? Wow!
**Bill:** Yeah, it was incredible. After the long climb up, we sat quietly for a while, admired the view and drank a great big bottle of water. We were really thirsty and then we started the long climb down again. The next day my legs really ached badly.
**Interviewer:** Good exercise, though!

**2 Interviewer:** Annette, can you tell us about an interesting experience you had on holiday?
**Annette:** An interesting experience? Oh, yeah, last December we went to China.
**Interviewer:** China? How interesting!
**Annette:** Yeah, it was. We went to Guilin and saw the famous mountains.
**Interviewer:** Oh yes, I've seen pictures of those mountains.
**Annette:** They really are amazing – tall and thin, just like needles. Well, one day we took a boat along the River Li. It was very misty in the morning and the water level was very low. At first, we could only just see the mountains outlined faintly against the pale sky. Later, the sun shone more brightly and the mountains rose majestically all around us. It was very quiet. The only noise we could hear was the boat scraping loudly on the bottom of the river. We watched Chinese fishermen on narrow rafts with big birds – cormorants – standing quietly beside them. And on command, the birds dived quickly into the water and caught fish for the fishermen. The birds couldn't eat the fish because they had string tied tightly around their necks.
**Interviewer:** Good heavens!

**3 Interviewer:** What about you, Marti? Did you have any interesting experiences when you were on holiday?
**Marti:** Sure did! One interesting experience was when I went to a small island called Rawa off the east coast of Malaysia.
**Interviewer:** Rawa? I've never heard of that. In Malaysia?
**Marti:** Yes. It was idyllic – like paradise! I took a boat from the Malaysian port of Mersing and, after nearly two hours of slowly chugging across the sea, we reached the island. I climbed carefully out of the boat onto an old wooden pier and took a look around me. The island looked deserted. The sea was turquoise and the white beach gleamed brightly in the sun. Palm trees swayed gracefully above a few wooden beach huts ... ahh!
**Interviewer:** It sounds wonderful!
**Marti:** Mmmm. I stayed for one whole week and learned to snorkel. When I was hungry, a Malaysian boy climbed up a palm tree to get me a fresh coconut. I didn't know such places existed.

## Review 2 Exercise 1

Yes, my job is always very busy. I usually start at 8.30 in the morning, but I often get in much earlier when there's a lot to do. Sometimes I start at 7.00. My boss, Helen, generally comes in before 9.00 am.

The first thing I always do is check Helen's diary so I can tell her about important meetings and get out the papers she needs for them. Helen likes coffee in the morning, but I don't usually make it for her. She gets it herself. She's good like that! I hate serving coffee!

Next, I always ask her if she has any letters to dictate. Sometimes this takes a couple of hours. By this time,

the post has usually arrived, so I check it and open it and direct it to the staff concerned. Most of the post is usually for Helen, though, so I look at it carefully and get out any documents Helen needs to deal with. After that, I often spend the day typing letters, answering the telephone, organising her schedule. Anything can happen! One thing I must always do at some point during the day is go through all the newspapers and cut out any interesting articles or reports on our clients or our own company. Occasionally, I go with her to see a new client. It's possible for me to go with Helen on business trips abroad, but this is rare. I'd like to go more often.

I don't always manage to get a lunch break, so I usually bring something to eat to work with me so I can eat at my desk. I don't mind. I generally finish work between 6.00 and 6.30. It's a long day, but I enjoy my job. Helen's a good boss, but she definitely needs me to organise her!

## Unit 11 Exercise 2

**1 Carmen:** Oh no. This queue is very slow, isn't it?
**Woman:** Yes, I know what you mean. It's always the same in this shop.
**Carmen:** Mmm. That queue looks quicker, doesn't it?
**Woman:** Yes. Oh, we're moving now.
**Carmen:** Thank goodness. Oh, that's a lovely cake you've got there!
**Woman:** Eh? Oh, yes, it is, isn't it? It's my son's birthday tomorrow.
**Carmen:** How nice.
**Woman:** Yes. He'll be three.
**Carmen:** Well, I hope he enjoys the cake.
**Woman:** He will ... Oh, look, it's your turn.
**Carmen:** Thanks. See you again maybe!
**Woman:** Yes, see you.

**2 Carmen:** Hello, I'm Carmen. You're John's father, aren't you? John's expecting me.
**Parent:** Hello. Yes. Come in. He's nearly ready.
**Carmen:** Thanks. Oh, it's nice and warm in here!
**Parent:** Yes, it's a bit cold tonight. I don't suppose you like this weather!
**Carmen:** No, not really. Oh, what a lovely room! It's so cosy.
**Parent:** Mmm. Thanks.
**Carmen:** You like football!
**Parent:** Mmm.
**Carmen:** Right. So, er, what team do you support?
**Parent:** Oh ... West Ham ... they're playing now.
**Carmen:** Oh yes, so they are. Mmmm. Who's winning?
**Parent:** Not sure yet. Oh, here's John. Have a lovely time.
**John:** Hi Carmen.
**Carmen:** Hi John. Bye. It was nice meeting you!
**Parent:** Yes. Mind how you go.
**Carmen and John:** Yes.

**3 Carmen:** Hello, Mrs Wallace. How are you?
**Neighbour:** Eh? Oh hello, dear. Fine, thanks. Just going to the shops, are you?
**Carmen:** Er, no, I'm going to my English class.
**Neighbour:** Really? That's nice.
**Carmen:** Mmm, yes.
**Neighbour:** Lovely day, isn't it?
**Carmen:** Mmm ... a bit cold for me, I'm afraid. By the way, how's the dog?
**Neighbour:** Oh much better, thanks. He saw the vet yesterday. He's still got to have three different sorts of tablets and ...
**Carmen:** Oh, look at the time! I must be going ...
**Neighbour:** ... an injection ... Oh, yes, dear, OK. Nice to see you.
**Carmen:** Yes, take care. Bye.
**Neighbour:** Bye.

**4 Carmen:** What a lovely baby! She's beautiful!
**Woman:** He. Yeah, thanks.
**Carmen:** How old is he?
**Woman:** Six months, three days and ten hours.
**Carmen:** Really? What's his name?
**Woman:** Nugent.
**Carmen:** Nugent? What a nice name! He looks a real little devil!
**Woman:** Oh, he's a real little devil, all right ... aren't you, Nu Nu?

**Carmen:** Well, must go. It was nice talking to you both.
**Woman:** Likewise. Bye.
**Carmen:** Bye. Bye, Nougat!
**Woman:** Nugent!

## Unit 11 Exercise 5(b)

**Man:** Hello, love! Cheer up!
**Carmen:** Pardon?
**Man:** You look so miserable!
**Carmen:** Do I?
**Man:** You're not from round here, are you?
**Carmen:** No, I'm from Chile.
**Man:** Chile! Really? That's a long way.
**Carmen:** Yes.
**Man:** Would you like a drink, love?
**Carmen:** No, thank you.
**Man:** Oh, go on. It'll cheer you up!
**Carmen:** I said no thank you. Look, I'm waiting for a friend.
**Man:** I'll be your friend.
**Carmen:** Please leave me alone.
**Man:** Oh, don't be like that!
**Carmen:** Go away. I'm not interested.
**Man:** All right, OK, OK ...

## Unit 12 Exercise 2

**Pat:** Hello?
**Mike:** Hello. Is that Pat?
**Pat:** Yes, speaking.
**Mike:** Oh, hi! This is Mike. You know, Mike Hallam. We met at Bill's last week.
**Pat:** Oh yes ... how nice of you to call. How are you?
**Mike:** Er, fine, fine. Are you busy right now? I'm not interrupting, am I?
**Pat:** No, no, I'm just watching TV.
**Mike:** Er, well, I was wondering ... what are you doing next week?
**Pat:** Next week? When?
**Mike:** Um, well, I've been invited to a party next Saturday and I was wondering whether you'd like to come with me. That is, if you're free.
**Pat:** Saturday? Well, I'd love to, but I'm afraid I can't. I'm going to Paris for the weekend.
**Mike:** Oh, dear, what a shame ... I hope you have a nice time.
**Pat:** Yes, thanks. Listen, how about going to the cinema one night this week?
**Mike:** Oh yeah, great! Let's do that.
**Pat:** Do you fancy the new De Niro film? It's on at the Roxy.
**Mike:** Mmm, yeah. That'd be super. It's had good reviews, hasn't it? What night would you like to go?
**Pat:** Wednesday?
**Mike:** Oh, I'm sorry, I can't on Wednesday. My kids are coming over. But I could go on Thursday, though ...

## Unit 13 Exercise 3

**Mariko:** Excuse me, I wonder if you could help me?
**Person 1:** Yes?
**Mariko:** I'm trying to get to Nurses Walk. Could you tell me how to get there, please?
**Person 1:** Sorry. I'm a stranger here myself!
**Mariko:** Oh, sorry.

**Mariko:** Excuse me.
**Person 2:** Yes?
**Mariko:** I wonder if you could help me?
**Person 2:** Yes?
**Mariko:** Um ... Could you tell me how to get to Nurses Walk from here, please?
**Person 2:** Nurses Walk? Er ... just a minute, let me think. Yes. You've come too far.
**Mariko:** Too far?
**Person 2:** Yes, go back and turn left and then go past the pub. The Fortune of War. Then you turn left through the archway and ...
**Mariko:** Sorry? What is archw...?
**Person 2:** Archway. It's like a gateway with a round top. Here, look, it's in your guidebook.
**Mariko:** Oh yes. Ah! So I go through the archway! Ah! I didn't know 'archway'.

**Person 2:** You missed it.
**Mariko:** Yes. So stupid!
**Person 2:** OK, so, go through the archway and then turn right and you're there.
**Mariko:** Through the archway and turn right. Thank you very, very much.
**Person 2:** No worries! You're welcome.

## Unit 14 Exercise 2

**Jean:** Turn right . . . and it's the third door on the left. Oh yes. Here it is.
**Cathie:** Here we go . . .
**Stavros:** I'll get it! Hi!
**Jean:** Hi, Stavros! Hope we're not too late.
**Stavros:** No, no.
**Cathie:** Here you are, we've brought some wine.
**Stavros:** Hey, thanks. You didn't have to do that! Come in. Let me take your things.
**Cathie:** Thanks.
**Jean:** Nice place you've got here! Oh hi, Ari!
**Ari:** Jean! Cathie! I'm so glad you came.
**Cathie:** We're a bit late. Your directions weren't very clear.
**Ari:** Never mind. Come in, sit down.
**Jean and Cathie:** Thanks.
**Jean:** What a lovely view!
**Cathie:** Wow! You can see the river.
**Ari:** Yes, it's nice, isn't it? Let me get you a drink. Jean, what would you like?
**Jean:** Could I have a glass of white wine, please?
**Ari:** We've got some retsina. You must try it! It's great.
**Jean:** Er, well, OK then, yes please.
**Ari:** Well, you don't have to drink it if you don't like it. Would you like some retsina, too, Cathie?
**Cathie:** Er, no thanks. Not for me. I'd like a glass of water, please.
**Ari:** Water? OK. Stav, one retsina and one glass of water, please.
**Stavros:** OK.
**Cathie:** What was that?
**Stavros:** Nothing, ha ha, nothing . . . it's OK.
**Ari:** Would you like some nuts?
**Jean:** Oh, yes, please.
**Cathie:** Maybe later. Er . . . Ari, could I use your phone, please?
**Ari:** Yes, of course, it's in the kitchen.
**Cathie:** Thanks. I'll be quick.
**Jean:** Her mother's not well. Hey, this is a very nice flat. May I have a look round?
**Ari:** Sure! Let me show you my bedroom.
**Jean:** Ari! Oh, Cathie. Everything OK?
**Cathie:** Yes, thanks. Ari, may I use your bathroom?
**Ari:** Certainly. It's the second door on the right.
**Cathie:** Thanks.
**Stavros:** Here's your retsina, Jean.

## Unit 14 Exercise 5

**Jean:** This is delicious! Did you make it yourself, Ari?
**Ari:** Thanks. Yes, I did.
**Cathie:** You're a fantastic cook!
**Ari:** Not really . . . well, thanks.
**Stavros:** Mmm. Would you like some more, Cathie?
**Cathie:** Oh, yes, I would!
**Stavros:** Here you are.
**Cathie:** Thanks.
**Ari:** What about you, Jean?
**Jean:** Ooh, no thanks. Not for me. I'm full, thanks. It was lovely.

## Unit 14 Exercise 6

**Cathie:** I'm afraid I must be going. I have to get to work early tomorrow.
**Jean:** Mmm, me too.
**Stavros:** Oh no! Don't you want to see that video?
**Jean:** Oh, the video!
**Cathie:** What was it again?
**Stavros:** 'Some Like It Hot', you know, with Marilyn Monroe.
**Jean:** Oh, I love that film!
**Ari:** Yes, me too.
**Cathie:** Oh, well, Jean, you stay, if you want, but I must be going.

**Jean:** Well . . . No, no, I must go, too.
**Ari:** What a shame! Are you sure you won't stay . . . ?
**Jean:** I'm sorry, we really must be going now.
**Stavros:** Right. I'll get your coats.
**Jean:** It's been a lovely evening. Thanks for having us!
**Cathie:** Yes, thanks for the delicious meal. I really enjoyed it.
**Stavros:** You're welcome! I hope you'll come again.
**Ari:** Yes, do.
**Jean:** No, next time, you can come to my place. I'll cook!
**Stavros:** Great!
**Jean:** I'll give you a call.
**Cathie:** Bye, thanks again!
**Stavros and Ari:** Bye! Bye! See you!

## Unit 15 Exercise 3

**Stavros:** Hello?
**Jean:** Hello? Is that Ari?
**Stavros:** No, this is Stavros.
**Jean:** Oh, hi, this is Jean.
**Stavros:** Oh, hi, Jean. How are you?
**Jean:** Fine, thanks. You?
**Stavros:** Yeah, yeah . . .
**Jean:** Is Ari there?
**Stavros:** Oh . . . er . . . no, I'm afraid he's gone out.
**Jean:** Oh. I see. When will he be in?
**Stavros:** I don't really know, Jean.
**Jean:** OK. Stavros, could you give him a message, please?
**Stavros:** Sure. Just a moment. Let me get a pen. OK.
**Jean:** OK. Tell him I called to ask him if he'd like to come to the Opera with me on Saturday.
**Stavros:** Wow! Which opera?
**Jean:** La Bohème. At the Royal Opera House.
**Stavros:** Lucky man!
**Jean:** Tell him I have to know by tomorrow morning at the latest.
**Stavros:** Tomorrow morning. OK. I'll tell him.
**Jean:** By 8 am!
**Stavros:** Hmmm. Look, Jean, he's gone to see a friend. Maybe you could call him there as it's urgent.
**Jean:** Friend? Er . . . OK. What's the number?
**Stavros:** Hold on. It's 998 2765.
**Jean:** 998 27 . . . ?
**Stavros:** 65.
**Jean:** Right, Stavros. Thanks.
**Stavros:** OK, bye.
**Jean:** Bye!

## Unit 15 Exercise 4

**Nina:** Hello? Nina speaking.
**Jean:** Oh, er, hello. Is er, Ari there, please?
**Nina:** Ari? Who shall I say it is?
**Jean:** This is a friend of his, Jean.
**Nina:** Ari's friend? Hold on, I'll ask him if he wants to speak to you.
**Jean:** Hmm!
**Nina:** Ari, darling. Someone called Jean for you . . .
**Ari:** Jean? Oh . . . er right. Hello, Jean. How are you?
**Jean:** Ari! Who's Nin . . . ?
**Ari:** Sorry Jean, I didn't quite catch that! Nina please!
**Jean:** I said who's Nina?
**Ari:** Oh, just a student from the college.
**Jean:** I see . . . just helping her with her homework, are you?
**Ari:** Sorry? What did you say?
**Jean:** Oh, nothing. Ari . . . ?
**Ari:** What?
**Jean:** Look, oh never mind! I'll talk to you another time.
**Ari:** Jean?
**Jean:** Bye.
**Ari:** Goodbye.

## Unit 15 Exercise 5

**Reception:** Pratt's Hotel. Good evening.
**Ari:** Good evening. Could you put me through to reservations, please?
**Reception:** Certainly, sir. Just a moment. Putting you through now.
**Ari:** Thanks.

**Rservations:** Reservations. Can I help you?
**Ari:** Yes, I'm calling to make a reservation for a double room for two nights in May.
**Reseption:** Yes, sir. When exactly were you thinking of?
**Ari:** 21st and 22nd.
**Reception:** Just a moment, sir. Yes, that's fine. Could I have your name, please?
**Ari:** Yes . . . Petropoulos.
**Reception:** I beg your pardon, sir? Could you spell that, please?
**Ari:** Yes, it's P-E-T-R-O-P-O-U-L-O-S.
**Reception:** Thank you, sir.
**Ari:** Right. Er . . . how much will that cost?
**Reception:** The room is £160 per night plus VAT.
**Ari:** OK. Thank you.
**Reception:** Thank you for calling, sir. Goodbye.
**Ari:** Goodbye.

## Review 3 Exercise 1

**Carmen:** The train's late again, I see!
**Stranger:** Yeah. Terrible, isn't it?
**Carmen:** Mmm. I wonder what the excuse is this time? Leaves on the track?
**Stranger:** Yeah, probably.
**Carmen:** Maybe it's a signal failure.
**Stranger:** We had that yesterday.
**Carmen:** Oh.
**Stranger:** Last week it was the snow. Before that it was a bomb alert.
**Carmen:** Yes, there's always something, isn't there?

## Unit 16 Exercise 2

**Chris:** What should we take to this picnic, then, do you think?
**Alan:** I thought maybe some nice French cheese.
**Chris:** Oh yes, and some French bread to go with it.
**Alan:** Mmm.
**Chris:** What else?
**Alan:** How about some ham?
**Chris:** OK . . . and some of those wonderful stuffed olives.
**Alan:** Oh yes! Let's get some paté, too.
**Chris:** Duck paté! Mmm. And some rolls.
**Alan:** How many?
**Chris:** Er, half a dozen. Bacon, lettuce, tomato?
**Alan:** Yes, and tuna.
**Chris:** Tuna rolls?
**Alan:** Yes.
**Chris:** OK.
**Alan:** We should take something to drink, too.
**Chris:** Yeah. Coke? Pepsi?
**Alan:** Let's get a carton of orange juice.
**Chris:** No, I prefer apple juice.
**Alan:** OK.
**Chris:** Come on, then, let's go. We can get all that from the deli on Duke Street.
**Alan:** Mmm, let's get a couple of bunches of grapes, too.

## Unit 16 Exercise 5

1  **Alan:** Hi! We'd like some French cheese, please.
**Assistant:** Well, we have a selection here for you to try. Help yourselves.
**Alan:** Thanks. Let's try the goat's cheese. Hmm. Phwor! It smells really strong.
**Chris:** Pooh, yuck . . . It's too strong for me. No, let's try the brie.
**Alan:** It looks too soft.
**Chris:** No, it tastes great. Mmm. Creamy. Try it.
**Alan:** Mmm. Not bad. Try the camembert.
**Chris:** Mmm. No, it's less creamy than the brie.
**Alan:** Yeah, you're right – it isn't soft enough, is it?
**Chris:** No.
**Alan:** OK, let's take some brie. How much?
**Chris:** Oh, how about a nice big piece?
**Assistant:** Like this, madam?
**Chris:** Yes, please.
**Alan:** Oh, look, avocados! Don't they look nice!
**Chris:** Feel them.
**Alan:** Mmm, this one's too hard. This one's a bit softer. No, they all feel too hard.
**Chris:** OK, never mind, then. Let's get the grapes.
**Assistant:** The red ones are very good, madam. Here.

**Chris:** Mmm, nice! Can I try one of those white grapes?
**Assistant:** Certainly. Here.
**Chris:** Oh yes, they taste sweeter.
**Alan:** Mmm, yes. The red ones aren't as nice as the white ones.
**Chris:** Yes. Let's have two big bunches.
**Alan:** Fine.

2   It's too hard!                   It's too sour!
    It's much too hard!            It's far too sour!
    It isn't soft enough!         It's not sweet enough!
    It's not soft enough!        It just isn't sweet enough!
    It really isn't soft
    enough!

## Unit 17 Exercise 3

**Pete:** So, er, what do you think?
**Sandra:** Oh, very nice. Yes, very nice.
**Waiter:** The menu, sir, madam.
**Pete:** Thank you.
**Sandra:** Thanks.
**Waiter:** Would you like to order your drinks now?
**Pete:** Sandra? What would you like?
**Sandra:** Well, . . .
**Pete:** Go on . . . have a drink.
**Sandra:** Er, yes, a mineral water, please.
**Pete:** OK, a mineral water and, er, an apple juice for me, please.
**Waiter:** Yes, sir.
**Pete:** Well, let's have a look, shall we? I think you'll be impressed.
**Sandra:** Mmm. Looks good.
**Pete:** Would you like a starter?
**Sandra:** Mmm.
**Pete:** I had the artichokes here last time. They were the most delicious thing on the menu!
**Sandra:** Really? You obviously know this place well! I'd love some oysters. Do you think they've got any oysters?
**Pete:** Let's ask. Er . . . excuse me? Waiter?
**Waiter:** Yes, sir? Are you ready to order now?
**Pete:** Er, no. My friend was wondering if you have any oysters today.
**Waiter:** Oysters? I'm afraid not, sir, but the caviare is delicious.
**Sandra:** Oh.
**Pete:** Thanks.
**Sandra:** Never mind. I'll have the pancake with caviare, then.
**Pete:** OK, I'll go for the artichokes again. They were wonderful.
**Sandra:** Hmm. Oh, look, what's that?
**Pete:** Where?
**Sandra:** There, the man in the dark suit. What's he got?
**Pete:** Oh, that looks like the avocado and lime salad.
**Sandra:** It looks really appetising, doesn't it? Oh and look at the dessert trolley! Look at those lovely creamy cakes!
**Pete:** I know. Great, isn't it? What would you like next?
**Sandra:** Oh, er, hmm, I can't decide . . . What do you recommend?
**Pete:** How about the veal with orange? It's the tastiest veal in town!
**Sandra:** Er no, actually, I'm a vegetarian.
**Pete:** Are you? I didn't know! Oh dear!
**Sandra:** Well, not really a vegetarian – I eat fish and some dairy products. But I don't eat any meat.
**Pete:** Oh, right. Well, there's some good fish on the menu.
**Sandra:** Hmm, no. I 'd like the curried vegetables.
**Pete:** That's quite hot and spicy, you know.
**Sandra:** Mm, yes, you're right. I know, I'll have the lobster thermidor.
**Pete:** Lobster! Oh, er, OK, if that's what you'd like. Vegetables?
**Sandra:** Oh, some salad and some rice, I think.
**Pete:** OK, well, I'll have the pork with lemon, French beans and new potatoes. Oh, you don't mind if I eat meat?
**Sandra:** No, no, of course not.
**Waiter:** Are you ready to order now, sir?
**Pete:** We haven't chosen our wine yet . . .
**Sandra:** Oh no . . .

## Unit 18 Exercise 2

1   **Man:** Oh, you're still awake!
    **Woman:** Mmm. How was work?
    **Man:** Terrible. You'll never guess what's happened.
    **Woman:** What? You sound dreadful! What's the matter?
    **Man:** I've lost my job.
    **Woman:** You've lost your job? What, got the sack?
    **Man:** Yes.
    **Woman:** Just like that? What have you done?
    **Man:** Nothing! Well, I had some trouble with a customer last night. He and his girlfriend or wife or whatever complained non-stop about the wine and the food and, well, everything. Finally, she started to choke on a bit of lobster and they wanted to rush her off to the hospital. I got him a taxi and then when I gave him the bill he went berserk. Anyway, he complained to the manager and I've lost my job.
    **Woman:** Oh, no! This is bad news. This is really bad news! What are we going to do now?
    **Man:** I'm sorry, love, I really am.

2   **Woman:** Oh, my God! Oh, no! Oh, I don't believe it!
    **Man:** What? What's the matter?
    **Woman:** You'll never guess what's happened. I've . . . I've lost my passport.
    **Man:** What! Surely not! Have you had a good look?
    **Woman:** Of course.
    **Man:** Look again. God knows, you carry so much around with you in that bag! Maybe it's at the bottom. Hell, that's *all* we need!
    **Woman:** *You* look! It's not there!
    **Man:** OK, OK, let's think. Have you seen it today?
    **Woman:** Er . . . yes. I had it out last night and then I put it in my bag this morning before we left the hotel.
    **Man:** Sure about that?
    **Woman:** Yes, definite.
    **Man:** Maybe you've left it in the Ladies in the restaurant. Did you take anything out of your bag?
    **Woman:** Ah! Maybe. I remember looking for my hairbrush . . .
    **Man:** Let's go back and see.

3   **Georgina:** Hello?
    **Operator:** Hello? Ms Pearce?
    **Georgina:** Yes.
    **Operator:** Los Angeles here. I have a collect call for you from a Mr Cross. Will you accept it?
    **Georgina:** Er . . . OK. Go ahead.
    **Roy:** Hello, hello? Georgina? It's me, Roy.
    **Georgina:** Why are you still in LA?
    **Roy:** You'll never guess what's happened . . . I've missed my flight! I'm sorry. I won't be back tomorrow.
    **Georgina:** Oh Roy! You twit! That's just wonderful! How did you do that? You know it's my birthday!
    **Roy:** Yes, I know and I'm really sorry. I got stuck in one hell of a traffic jam in downtown LA. Look, I've booked a room in the airport hotel and I've managed to get a seat on a late flight tomorrow. I should be in London by Wednesday lunchtime.
    **Georgina:** Wednesday?
    **Roy:** Yes. Sorry.
    **Georgina:** But I've booked theatre tickets for tomorrow night!
    **Roy:** Can you get them changed?
    **Georgina:** I'll try. If not, I'll go with someone else.
    **Roy:** Er . . . right. I'd better go. I'll get a taxi from Heathrow. See you on Wednesday. Er, happy birthday.
    **Georgina:** Yeah, thanks. See you.

## Unit 19 Exercise 2

**Martin:** Hello!
**Recording:** Hello. I'm sorry I can't come to the phone at the moment, but if you'd like to leave a message, please do so after the music and the silly voice. Thank you. Leave your message now!
**Martin:** Oh, oh dear, an answering machine! I didn't expect that! Well, er, oh, now you sound very . . . very nice! I hate talking to machines, don't you? Um, er, well now you don't actually know me. I've never done this before . . . I got your letter and . . . oh, no . . . I'm Martin and, er . . . oh dear. I'm Mar . . . Oh no, I've said that.

Oh no! That was awful! She won't want to meet me! Let's try the other one. Where's the letter? Oh, yes, here we are. Hmm.

**Recording:** Hello. This is Ogniana speaking. I am not at home now, so please leave a message and I will call you back as soon as I can. Thank you. Goodbye.
**Martin:** Ahem. Hello, you don't know me. My name is Martin Dodds. That's D-O-D-D-S. I, um, put an ad in the *Nottingham Post* and you sent me a reply. I was looking through the replies I got and I, er, I liked your letter a lot, so I was wondering whether we could talk. Look, I'll call you again tomorrow, OK? Perhaps we could talk then? Or you could call me. My number is 515152. That is 515152. I'm at home most evenings. Bye.

Phew! That was better. Hmm. Interesting voice. She sounded OK. Yeah.

## Unit 19 Exercise 4

**Martin:** Hello? Yes?
**Ogniana:** Oh, er, hello. This is Ogniana. You left a message on my answering machine today.
**Martin:** Oh, yes. Yes! Hello. It's very good of you to call back, I wasn't expecting you to call . . . I've never done this before, you see, and . . .
**Ogniana:** I'm sorry. Could you speak a little slower, please? My English isn't so good!
**Martin:** Eh? Oh, sorry. Yes, of course. But your English sounds good to me!
**Ogniana:** Oh. Thank you. You're very kind.
**Martin:** Not at all, not at all. I . . .
**Ogniana:** I'm sorry. What did you say?
**Martin:** Pardon? Oh, er, nothing, really. Now, I was wondering if we could have a little chat and get to know each other a bit and then, maybe, meet up. What do you think?
**Ogniana:** Er, yes, of course.
**Martin:** So, er, Ogniana, that's an unusual name! Where are you from?
**Ogniana:** I come from Bulgaria. Sofia, in fact. I told you in my letter.
**Martin:** Oh, right, yes. Hey, I was in your home town last summer. Had a great time. The people . . .
**Ogniana:** You were in Sofia last summer?
**Martin:** Yes, that's right.
**Ogniana:** Did you like it?
**Martin:** Oh yes, very much. I loved the architecture.
**Ogniana:** You loved the . . . ?
**Martin:** Architecture. The buildings in Sofia. Fantastic.
**Ogniana:** Oh yes. They're very nice.
**Martin:** Have you been here long?
**Ogniana:** Oh, 13 months now. I study at the university.
**Martin:** What are you studying?
**Ogniana:** Engineering.
**Martin:** Engineering? Oh yes, Nottingham's got a good reputation for that.
**Ogniana:** A good . . . ?
**Martin:** Reputation.
**Ogniana:** Oh yes. Yes, it is a very good course. I have some questions. What do you do?
**Martin:** Me? I'm an estate agent.
**Ogniana:** Sorry? What is 'estate agent'?
**Martin:** An estate agent is someone who sells houses.
**Ogniana:** Oh yes. I know.
**Martin:** So, er, Ogniana, what are your hobbies?
**Ogniana:** Sorry, I didn't quite catch that.
**Martin:** Your hobbies. What do you like doing?
**Ogniana:** I think I told you in my letter, didn't I?
**Martin:** Oh yes. You like dancing and eating and . . .
**Ogniana:** Eating, yes. In nice restaurants!
**Martin:** Right. Do you like Indian food?
**Ogniana:** Oh yes. Very much.
**Martin:** Well, how about meeting me for an Indian meal on Saturday night?
**Ogniana:** Mmmm. Yes. OK. Where?
**Martin:** We could meet at the Nur Jehan on Mansfield Road.
**Ogniana:** How do you spell it?
**Martin:** N-U-R – and then new word – J-E-H-A-N. It's on the Mansfield Road on the left as you come out of the centre of town.
**Ogniana:** Nur Jehan. On the Mansfield Road, on the left coming out of town.

**Martin:** That's right. We could meet at 7.30. I'll wear a black leather jacket.
**Ogniana:** I'll wear a black leather jacket, too.
**Martin:** Great.
**Ogniana:** OK, so that's ... 7.30 at the Nur Jehan on Mansfield Road on Saturday night.
**Martin:** Right.
**Ogniana:** Is that near the theatre?
**Martin:** No, not really.
**Ogniana:** Well, I'll get a taxi. Don't worry.
**Martin:** Fine. Well, see you then, then.
**Ogniana:** Yes. See you then. Goodbye.
**Martin:** Bye.

## Unit 20 Exercise 2(a)

**Interviewer:** Ellie's your first baby, isn't she?
**Karen:** Mmm, yes. She's six months old now.
**Interviewer:** All mothers dream about their children's future. What do you predict for Ellie? How do you see her life in, say, 25 years from now?
**Karen:** Well, I think about it a lot. I look at her little face and I think: will you get married and have babies of your own, will you be a mother or will you travel around the world and see things I've never seen?
**Interviewer:** Mmm.
**Karen:** You see, the world will be very different when she's a young woman. There'll be even fewer jobs than there are now and women will have to be very strong and hard-working if they want a career. I think Ellie will be very tough. She has a very strong personality! Oh yes. Oh, I'm sure she'll get a good job, probably in something creative, like her father, Phil. He's a graphic designer, in advertising. First, though, she'll go to university. Maybe she'll live overseas for a year or two to get more experience. I did that. I think it was very important. She'll be successful in her work and make a lot of money! Well, I hope so, anyway.
**Interviewer:** Do you think she'll get married?
**Karen:** Maybe she will. She'll have lots of boyfriends, anyhow. She's very pretty now and I think she'll be terribly attractive when she grows up. She won't be short, like me. She's got long legs already, like Phil. I think she'll be quite sporty, too.
**Interviewer:** What about children? Will you be a grandma?
**Karen:** Hmm. Yes, I expect I will be ... gosh, what a thought!

## Unit 20 Exercise 5

**Interviewer:** So, you're retiring next month. How does it feel?
**Phil:** Well, OK. It'll be a very different life for me, of course.
**Interviewer:** What are you going to do?
**Phil:** Well, my wife, Karen, died last year ...
**Interviewer:** Oh dear, I'm sorry.
**Phil:** Yes, thank you ... and I don't want to stay in our house on my own, so I'm going to move soon to a bungalow in Essex, to be nearer to my daughter, Ellie, and her husband. I'm going to join the British Legion there – that's an organisation and a club for ex-service people – I was in the army for a while when I was young. Yes, so, I'm going to join the British Legion and get to know people there. It'll be a good way to make friends, I think.
**Interviewer:** What about hobbies? Are you going to take up any new hobbies?
**Phil:** Oh yes, but not a new hobby. I'm going to start painting again. I like doing water colours. I'm going to try oil painting, too. I'm going to read a lot, too. All the books I never had time to read before!
**Interviewer:** Sounds great! Anything else?
**Phil:** Oh, yes, I'm going to go on holiday to Greece with my daughter and her husband, probably in August. That'll be nice. We're going to fly to Athens, then take a cruise around some islands.
**Interviewer:** Lovely!

## Acknowledgements

**The author wishes to thank the following people for their help in the production of this course:**

Peter Donovan for his guidance, support and encouragement; my editors, James Dingle and Meredith Levy, for their professionalism, hard work, excellent editing skills and cheerful, supportive demeanour; Denise Quinton and Kathryn Wong for their innovative design and great sense of humour; Anne Colwell for her design management; the illustrators for providing colour and chuckles.

Gregory Hoehner for his contribution to the Self-study Workbook; Rob Heath for his work on the Grammar Review; all the people who have allowed us to use their photographs and names; all the people who gave their time to appear in photographs; James Richardson, the actors and all at Studio AVP for the recordings.

Philip Sinclair for providing me with emotional and physical assistance in times of need; friends and ex-colleagues from the British Council in Singapore, especially Linda Hanington, for their support and advice; Norman Whitney and Philip Prowse for their useful comments; all the ELT professionals from whom we received feedback during the piloting stage of this course; 'Derek' and all other sources of inspiration.

This course is dedicated to Philip William James Sinclair.

**The author and publishers would like to thank the following individuals and institutions for their help in writing reports, testing the material and for the invaluable feedback which they provided:**

Susan Garvin, Bauffe, Belgium; Ricardo Sili da Silva, Cultura Inglesa, Rio de Janeiro, Brazil; Jiřina Babáková, Mladá Boleslav, Czech Republic; LS-Kieliopisto, Tampere, Finland; Diann Gruber, Champs sur Marne, France; Metaform-Langues, Chamalières, France; International House Language School, Budapest, Hungary; Wall Street Institute, Milan, Italy; Centro Linguistico di Ateneo, Parma, Italy; Tom Hinton, British Council Cambridge English School, Kyoto, Japan; Crown Institute of Studies, Auckland, New Zealand; Barbara Duff, British Council, Muscat, Oman; LINK, Gliwice, Poland; International House, Coimbra, Portugal; ELCRA-Bell, Geneva, Switzerland; Volkshochschule, Zürich, Switzerland; International House, Bangkok, Thailand; Roger Scott, Bournemouth, UK; Cambridge Academy of English, Cambridge, UK; Eurocentre, London, UK; Hampstead Garden Suburb Institute, London, UK; Jeremy Jacobson, Truro, UK.

**The author and publishers are grateful to the following illustrators and photographic sources:**

**Illustrators:** Matthew Cook: pp. 28, 63 *t*; Andrew Davidson: pp. 40-41; Ian Dicks: pp. 31, 35, 57, 59 *t*, 62, 63 *b*; Steve Gyapay: pp. 16 *t*, 46 *l*, 55; John Ireland: pp. 6 *l*, 44, 45 *l*, 61; John Lawrence: pp. 11, 14; Stephen May: pp. 6 *r*, 13, 30, 47, 70; Ron Mercer: pp. 15 *t*, 18 *r*, 27, 29, 45 *r*, 52, 66; Jill Newton: pp. 18 *l*, 21, 36, 50-51; Jenny Norton: p. 46 *r*; Lynne Russell: pp. 15 *b*, 22, 34; Meilo So: pp. 16 *b*, 24, 48, 58, 59 *b*.

Cover illustration by Rosemary Woods.

**Photographic sources:** James Davis Travel Photography: pp. 13 *t*, 16; Topham Picturepoint: pp. 13 *b*.

All other photographs taken by Steve Bond at F64.

*t* = top    *b* = bottom    *l* = left    *r* = right

Picture research by Sandie Huskinson-Rolfe of PHOTOSEEKERS.

Design by QuintonWong.